New Ideas on the World's Complexities

Also from Westphalia Press

westphaliapress.org

New Ideas on the World's Complexities

Vol. 1, No. 1 of Policy and Complex Systems

Edited by Mirsad Hadzikadic

WESTPHALIA PRESS
An imprint of Policy Studies Organization

New Ideas on the World's Complexities: Vol. 1, No. 1 of Policy and Complex Systems
All Rights Reserved © 2014 by Policy Studies Organization

Westphalia Press
An imprint of Policy Studies Organization
1527 New Hampshire Ave., NW
Washington, D.C. 20036
dgutierrezs@ipsonet.org

ISBN-13: 978-1-941472-91-0
ISBN-10: 1941472915

Updated material and comments on this edition
can be found at the Westphalia Press website:
www.westphaliapress.org

Policy and Complex Systems
Volume 1 Issue 1 Spring 2014

Table of Contents

Editor's Introduction

Welcome to the inaugural issue of the ***Journal on Policy and Complex Systems*** (***JPCS***). It is one of the first journals that promote application of complex systems theories, methods, models, and simulations in the domain of policy development, implementation, and evaluation. Policies are developed to regulate complex aspects of the society. However, policies and policy development process are in themselves a complex system. Therefore, it is only natural to offer a venue for exploration of policies as complex systems.

The ***JPCS*** will promote both quantitative and qualitative, complex systems-based, research in policy development. To that extent, models and simulations will be both encouraged and expected. We hope that over time a repository of models, simulations, and data sets will be created for the benefit of the entire community. In addition, novel approaches to communicating results and ideas will be encouraged, including YouTube video clips, graphic visualizations, and audio explorations.

This first issue includes six articles. They range from discussions on innovation and systems-of-systems approach to tools for policy analysis and policy making in information environments. Specifically, Juma revists Schumpeter in his analysis of innovation and development. Vinogradova and Serge probe the process of dissolution of a global alliance. Dombkins uses a system-of-systems approach to exploration of policy development. Ghorbani et al. explore the utility of agent-based modeling in policy analysis. Inguaggiato and Occelli use complexity as a paradigm for re-aligning government and governance relationships. Finally, Wagner and Kim explore the world of scientific publishing as a complex phenomenon. Future issues will address both focused themes and a broad treatment of policy and complexity issues.

It has been a remarkable journey from an idea for a journal to this first issue. There are many people who have been instrumental in making it possible. Paul Rich and Daniel Guiterrez-Sandoval of the journal publisher, Policy Studies Organization, have been extremely supportive, helpful, and constructive throughout the process. Liz Johnson worked tirelessly to make the journal possible. JPCS' Editorial Board members have been exceptionally generous with their time commitment and advice. I have been humbled and blessed with the support of this extraordinary group of people.

On behalf of the entire ***JPCS*** team,

Mirsad Hadzikadic
University of North Carolina at Charlotte

Journal on Policy and Complex Systems
Letter to Editor

Congratulations on the emergence of the *Journal on Policy and Complex Systems* published by the Policy Studies Organization. It is refreshing to see such advances that assume an orientation toward the study of policy and complexity. As a social worker, I come from a discipline based on systems theories, yet our discipline remains too reliant on traditional experimental and quasi-experimental research methods. Given these circumstances, the creation of your journal addresses a significant void in the area of investigating social and welfare policy because this new outlet will allow for the greater dissemination of models that forecast the multiple effects resulting from modifying social policies.

Many of us in the fields of human services conducting policy research shifted to a to a complex adaptive systems (CAS) orientation perspective. This desire arose because traditional research approaches were insufficient, while it became apparent how this new perspective could better inform us through the development and manipulation of agent-based models (ABM). Several colleagues in social work and related human services disciplines are now experimenting with ABMs on how changing policy incentives and other boundaries can affect participation at both local and national levels.

Often too little is understood about how policy and incentives affect individual and family (agent) decisions as these agents seek resources and assistance to address their everyday needs. Through the use of CAS and ABMs many colleagues are beginning to better forecast how various social welfare policies and incentives affect behavior. As complexity increasingly is applied to a growing range of disciplines, I along with many others appreciate the efforts behind creating a scholarly journal addressing this growing perspective.

Sincerely,
Michael Wolf-Branigin, Associate Professor & Interim Chair
George Mason University – Department of Social Work

Journal on Policy and Complex Systems
Letter to the Editor

It is great to see a new journal devoted to complexity issues. There has never been a more important period than the present when the ideas and insights from complexity theory should be applied to policy. In the general readers eye complexity theory seems mysterious, abstract and basically inaccessible. This need not be the case. Basically, complexity theory says i) appreciate and influence general potentially desirable directions; ii) maximize flow of information and purposeful interactions; and iii) look for and rein in promising patterns and developments.

As my colleagues and I work on what we call the 'new pedagogies' (learning partnerships between and among students and teachers), link them to 'deep learning' (21st century skills and competencies), and see how both pedagogues and deep learning can be accelerated by technology, we see the application of complexity theory to be a perfect fit. We expect that such thinking will generate key insights for both policy and practice.

The inaugural issue of the Journal on Policy and Complex Systems looks like an exciting start. Each of the four articles tackles a big problem. It is especially noteworthy that the focus of the journal is on the linkage between complexity analysis, and specific policy developments.

I can't wait to read Schumpeter Revisited as well as the other articles which case a wide net for the work of complexity thinking and related policy. In every area of human kind there are growing difficulties of understanding what is happening and how we might obtain insights about what to do.

The digital world itself raises countless issues that ramify across every sector. I predict that this Journal will have a long and rich life with endless topics and cumulative insights. Bring on the debate and the widening of deliberation about policy and action!

Michael Fullan
Order of Canada, Professor Emeritus, OISE/University of Toronto.

Complexity, Innovation, and Development: Schumpeter Revisited

Calestous Juma[A]

The role of innovation and entrepreneurship is increasingly getting policy attention in emerging countries. A growing body of literature is deriving its inspiration from the work of Joseph Schumpeter. His seminal 1911 book, The Theory of Economic Development, outlined a general framework for understanding the role of innovation and entrepreneurship in economic transformation. Despite Schumpeter's influence on economic policies in industrialized countries, there has been little application of his work in emerging countries. On surface, the failure to apply Schumpeter's ideas to emerging countries appears to be an intellectual oversight. To the contrary, this paper argues that the application of Schumpeter's ideas to emerging countries was debated through the 1950s, but early architects of development studies deemed it to be irrelevant. The core of the rejection was an epistemological clash between Schumpeter's systems approach to economic transformation and that of his critics who adhered to a more static, linear, and incremental view of economic change. Thus, Schumpeter's central themes of innovation and entrepreneurship focused on endogenous transformation and evolution of economies, while his critics, who focused on the importance of central planning, relied on equilibrium models reflected in the role of bureaucracies as economic sources of stability.

Introduction[1]

Those seeking to bemoan the fate of emerging countries draw emblematic parallels with East Asian countries. One of the most evocative images is the claim that in the early 1960s Ghana and South Korea were at the same level of development. South Korea advanced to become an industrialized country now providing development assistance to Africa. Ghana, on the other hand, has gone through a serious of frustrating coups, economic stagnation, and negligible participation in the global trading system despite its gold mines and world-class cocoa plantations.

These cases conjure up images of a world of uneven growth dominated by inequities. Others have attributed the rise of East Asian economies to windfalls of the Cold War. But the seed of rapid economic transformation was planted in *The Theory of Economic Development*, Joseph Schumpeter's seminal work published in 1911. In this ground-breaking book Schumpeter outlined the epic role of innovation and entrepreneurship in economic development.[2] This was his bold attempt to depart from the

[A] Harvard Kennedy School

[1] This paper is drawn from the author's draft book tentatively entitled, *How Economies Succeed: Innovation and the Wealth of Nations*. I am grateful to Professor F.M. Scherer (Harvard Kennedy School) for sharing his insights and knowledge about Joseph Schumpeter that rekindled my interest to explore why Schumpeter's *Theory of Economic Development* only marginally informs policy discussions on "economic development." I have also benefited from valuable comments and additional information from Richard Nelson (Columbia University) and Norman Clark (The Open University, UK). Finally, I thank Katherine Gordon (Harvard Kennedy School) and Katharina Lix (Harvard College) for their research support for this paper.

[2] For an assessment of the evolution of Schumpeter's view of the relationships between innovation and entrepreneurship, see J. Hagedoorn, "Innovation and Entrepreneurship: Schumpeter Revisited," *Industrial and Corporate Change* 5 (3) (1996): 883-896.

theories of economic equilibrium that dominated classical economic text of the time.

Schumpeter's work was appropriately called "the theory of economic development" because it described a world that is analogous to large parts of today's emerging countries. However, these countries have not benefitted much from Schumpeter's intellectual legacy.

At first glance it would appear that the lack of application of Schumpeter's ideas to emerging countries was a historical oversight given that most of them were colonies at the time of his writing. However, these countries were desperately searching for alternative development models that would free them from dependence on their former colonial masters.

Schumpeter was writing during the ascendency of neoclassical economics that placed considerable emphasis on mathematical equilibrium models that Schumpeter was rejecting. Schumpeter framed economic development as an evolutionary process.[3] He laid the foundations of looking at economies as complex systems.[4] It is therefore not surprising that Schumpeter's work has been consistently excluded from compilations of studies on economic development, as surveyed by Thanawala.[5] In fact, the dismissal runs deep. Nobel laureate Arthur Lewis wrote in his 1955 book, *Theory of Economic Growth*, that Schumpeter's *Theory of Economic Development* "is very much narrower in scope than its title implies."[6]

This paper argues that although the work was not ignored, it was debated throughout much of the 1950s and the general consensus was that Schumpeter's ideas were not relevant to emerging countries. The paper traces the early debates in development studies on Schumpeter's ideas.

The paper is divided into four parts. The first part outlines the fundamental elements of Schumpeter's theory of development. This is followed by a review of debates on the relevance of Schumpeter's ideas in emerging countries. The third part assesses the evolution of development studies through the life of Hans Singer, a former student of Schumpeter and a leading architect of development theory and practice. The paper concludes with an assessment of policy implications of Schumpeter's relevance for contemporary economic policy in emerging countries.

The Economy as a Complex System

First, Schumpeter was concerned with overall system transformation in the same way that his critics wanted to see rapid economic change in emerging countries. He pioneered the application of complex systems thinking to economic development. Second, Schumpeter was interested in change over time, which is why he adopted an evolutionary approach that recognized the importance of history. By appealing to complexity and time, Schum-

---

[3] N. Clark, and C. Juma, *Long-Run Economics: An Evolutionary Theory of Economic Growth* (London: Pinter, 1992).

[4] M.C. Becker, T. Knudsen, and R. Swedberg, "Schumpeter's Theory of Economic Development: 100 Years of Development," *Journal of Evolutionary Economics*, 22, 5 (2012): 931.

[5] K. Thanawala, "Schumpeter's Theory of Economic Development and Development Economics," *Review of Social Economy*, 52, 4 (1994): 353–63.

[6] Quoted in D. Rimmer, "Schumpeter and the Underdeveloped Countries," *Quarterly Journal of Economics*, 75, 3 (August 1961): 422. When Ghana gained independence in 1957 Arthur Lewis became the country's first expatriate advisor and drew up its first five-year (1959–1963) development plan.

peter stood in sharp contrast with his critics whose economic models appealed to the static equilibrium notions although in practice they sought to depart from them.

Schumpeter's "economic sociology" is laid out in his "missing Chapter 7" of *The Theory of Economic Development*. The chapter, which was dropped in his 1926 edition of this book, laid out a summation of his theoretical outlook that emphasized the fact that economic development was an emergent property arising from endogenous systemic change and not a response to external stimuli. He stressed that "it is not possible to explain *economic* change by previous economic conditions alone. For the economic state of a people does not emerge simply from the preceding *economic* conditions, but only from the preceding total situation."[7]

Also evident in this formulation is the fact that economic evolution is a nonlinear or discontinuous process with emergent properties. Schumpeter saw "that kind of change arising from within the system *which so displaces its equilibrium point that the new one cannot be reached from the old one by infinitesimal steps*. Add successively as many mail coaches as you please, you will never get a railway thereby."[8] This theme is explicit in his notion of the generation of variety through new combinations as well as their selection and retention.

By adopting an ecosystem approach, Schumpeter was able to identify the forces of economic succession that resulted from the invasive waves of railroads.[9] For Schumpeter, "The essential point to grasp is that in dealing with capitalism we are dealing with an evolutionary process."[10] He continues, "[The] process of industrial mutation…that incessantly revolutionizes the economic structure *from within*, incessantly destroying the old one, incessantly creating a new one. This process of Creative Destruction is the essential fact about capitalism."[11]

A systems approach would make it easier, both conceptually and practically, to address the ecological implications of development. So far the dominant approaches to environmental issues came from the traditional conservation movement that assumes that the environment is better protected by excluding human activities. Efforts to promote sustainable development can hardly be advanced without a greater use of innovation.[12]

Schumpeter's dynamic theory of economic development continues to be marginalized in mainstream economics.[13] Schumpeter held the view that it was possible for one "to accept both his theory of

---

[7] Schumpeter, *The Theory of Economic Development*, 58 (emphasis in original).

[8] Ibid., 64 n. 1 (emphasis in original).

[9] See E.S. Andersen, "Railroadization as Schumpeter's Standard Case: An Evolutionary-Ecological Account," *Industry and Innovation* 9 (1–2) (2002),: 41–78.

[10] Schumpeter, *Capitalism, Socialism and Democracy*, 82.

[11] Ibid., 83.

[12] For a review of the role of innovation in sustainability, see S. Jacobsson and A. Bergek, "Innovation System Analyses and Sustainability Transitions: Contributions and Suggestions for Research," *Environmental Innovation and Societal Transitions* 1(1) (2011): 41–57; A. Smith et al., "Innovation Studies and Sustainability Transitions: The Allure of the Multi-Level Perspective and its Challenges," *Research Policy* 39(4) (2010): 435–448; and X. Fu and J. Zhang, "Technology Transfer, Indigenous Innovation and Leapfrogging in Green Technology: The Solar-PV Industry in China and India," *Journal of Chinese Economic and Business Studies* 9 (4) (2011): 329–347.

[13] See R. Nelson, "Why Schumpeter Has Had So Little Influence on Today's Main Line Economics, and Why This May Be Changing," Journal of Evolutionary Economics 22 (5) (November 2012): 902.

innovation-driven economic progress, and the equilibrium analysis of how markets determined prices and the allocation of resources."[14] But as Nelson rightly says, this "coexistence was incoherent."[15] Schumpeter's theory of innovation-driven economic development "not only put forth a different view of what was most important about capitalist economies. It diverged from theory that stressed equilibrium conditions.... It was virtually impossible to buy conceptually into both at the same time."[16]

Schumpeter was aware that a departure from equilibrium thinking would put him at odds with the economics establishment. His first book, *The Nature and Content of Theoretical Economics*, published in 1908 when he was 25, was a failure. His own mentor, Eugen von Böhm-Bawerk, advised him that knowledge did not advance through bright new insights but "through the old professors' dying off."[17]

Schumpeter did not wait. He proceeded to push the frontiers of economic thought with the publication of *The Theory of Economic Development*. The book challenged then current economic wisdom and was not well received from the outset.[18]

The central idea of Schumpeter's new book is that when "new combinations appear discontinuously, then the phenomenon characterising development emerg-es... Development in our sense is then defined by the carrying out of new combinations."[19] Schumpeter contends that "new combinations are, as a rule, embodied, as it were, in new firms which generally do not arise out of the old ones but start producing beside them...in general it is not the owner of stage-coaches who builds railways."[20] He did not consider the revival of new industries following downturns as necessarily representing innovation although such acts may create opportunities for innovation or the creation of new combinations. Indeed, Schumpeter notes that "[a]s a rule the new combinations must draw the necessary means of production from some old combinations."[21] What is critical, however, is the generation of novelty and not simply the return to previous levels of production.

Schumpeter's theory of development covers at least four key elements. First, he considers the process of economic development to be endogenous and driven by the creation of new combinations including new products, new production methods or processes, new organizational forms, new markets, and new sources of raw materials and inputs. Second, these combinations are carried out by entrepreneurs who are motivated to undertake certain actions. Third, the entrepreneur is the change agent whose actions disturb the equilibrium of the

---

[14] Ibid., 902.

[15] Ibid., 902.

[16] Ibid., 903.

[17] J.A. Schumpeter, *History of Economic Analysis* (New York: Oxford University Press, 1964), 850, quoted in McCraw, *Prophet of Innovation*, 63.

[18] As Schumpeter later recollected, "When this book first appeared in 1911, both the general view of the economic process embodied in and about half a dozen of the results it tried to establish seemed to many people so strikingly uncongenial and so far removed from traditional teaching that it met almost universal hostility." Letter from Schumpeter to David T. Pottinger, June 3, 1934, quoted in Becker, Knudsen, and Swedberg, "Schumpeter's Theory of Economic Development," 919.

[19] J.A. Schumpeter, *The Theory of Economic Development* (Cambridge, MA: Harvard University Press, 1934), 66.

[20] Schumpeter, *The Theory of Economic Development*, 66.

[21] Ibid., 68.

steady state and cause economic discontinuities. Finally, the emergence of credit-providing institutions plays a key role in stimulating entrepreneurial activities. In his view, it is the credit-providing institutions that take risks by providing funding to entrepreneurs.

Debating Schumpeter

The debate over the relevance of Schumpeter's theory to emerging countries started with the publication of Ragnar Nurkse's 1953 book, *Problems of Capital Formation in Underdeveloped Countries*. The timing is particularly important. Many of the major development planning efforts initiated by the United Nations (UN) and other international development agencies were just starting to take shape.[22] Nurkse is recognized as one of the founding fathers of classical development economics who worked with the League of Nations on the transition from peace to war. He was an advocate of a "big push" for large-scale investment in emerging countries to start and sustain the development process.

In grappling with the issue of emerging countries, he argued that "Schumpeter's theory seems to…provide the mould which we must use, although we may use it with slightly different ingredients."[23] He based his reasoning on the important role that Schumpeter assigns to "the creative entre-preneur, or rather to the action of considerable numbers of such entrepreneurs and their imitators, carrying out innovations, putting out new commodities, and devising new combinations of productive factors."[24]

Nurkse was particularly interested in the capital formation impact of the diffusion of technology across different industries. "Even if an innovation tends each time to originate in one particular industry, the monetary effects of the initial investment…are such as to promote a wave of new applications of capital over a range of different industries."[25] He drew inspiration from Schumpeter's contention that it is the "avalanche of consumers' goods that permanently deepens and widens the stream of real income although in the first instance they spell disturbance, losses, and unemployment."[26]

Nurkse believed that a "frontal attack" with "a wave of capital investments in a number of different industries…can economically succeed while any substantial application of capital by an individual entrepreneur in any particular industry may be blocked or discouraged by the limitations of the pre-existing market."[27] He envisaged that such an approach would create conditions for mutual support among a diverse range of entrepreneurs.

Nurkse recognized the importance of modifying Schumpeter's ideas to suit new geographical locations. He pointed out that defeating the forces that reinforce

---

[22] See, for example, A. Staples, *The Birth of Development: How the World Bank, Food and Agriculture Organization, and World Health Organization Changed the World, 1945–1965* (Kent, OH: Kent State University Press, 2006).

[23] R. Nurkse, *Capital Formation in Underdeveloped Countries* (New York: Oxford University Press, 1953),12.

[24] Ibid.,13.

[25] Ibid.,13.

[26] J.A. Schumpeter, *Capitalism, Socialism and Democracy* (New York: HarperCollins, 1942; reprint, with an introduction by Thomas K. McCraw, 2008), 68.

[27] Nurkse, *Capital Formation in Underdeveloped Countries*, 13.

economic stagnation may require different forms of institutional organization. "In the early industrial development of Japan, for instance, the state was the great innovator and the industrial pioneer on a wide front. Japan's early industrial development seems to have been 'planned' and carried out in large measure by the state."[28]

Schumpeter provided Nurkse with the vision to articulate a strategy for emerging countries that would entrust development in the hands of entrepreneurs. He was well aware of the debate between planners and anti-planners. His position was pragmatic, believing that "one cannot realistically treat the problem as...exclusive choice between state action and individual enterprise."[29] He was primarily concerned with capital formation and saw greater potential for reinvestment in the hands of entrepreneurs.[30]

Prior to the release of Nurkse's book, a forceful attack on Schumpeter was unleashed by Henry Wallich, an American central banker, economist, and Yale professor at the Third Meeting of Central Bank Technicians of the American Continent held in Havana, Cuba, in 1952. Wallich acknowledged that Schumpeter provided "the most outstanding intellectual performance" because of the internal coherence in his work, but argued that "in applying this doctrine to the less developed countries of our day, we find that it does not fit."[31] Wallich stressed that entrepreneurs as agents of change did not apply to less developed countries because the "entrepreneur is not the main driving force, innovation is not the most characteristic process, and private enrichment is not the dominant goal."[32]

For Wallich, countries differed in their national endowment for entrepreneurial qualities, which to some degree accounted for their economic stagnation.[33] He attributed this to this list of "human traits": "Real estate mindedness, mistrust of industrial ventures, remnants of a feudal past."[34] His authority was international agency surveys of missions. Although he acknowledged that Schumpeterian development could follow the rise of entrepreneurship, he remained pessimistic about its emergence.[35] This position is in contradiction with Nurkse, who noted that the "state might withdraw from areas where individual enterprise has learned to stand on its own feet and turn its attention to other fields where its powers are needed to clear the way."[36]

Wallich extended his objection to two other areas. He contended that innovation was not a characteristic feature of less-developed countries. For him, the

---

[28] Ibid., 15.

[29] Ibid., 155.

[30] "Leaving investment to the individual entrepreneur can have the advantage of providing the machinery for saving the increment of income which capital investment creates. If there is any hope for substantial private saving it lies mainly in the reinvestment of entrepreneurial profits." Ibid., 155.

[31] H.C. Wallich, "Some Notes Towards a Theory of Derived Development," in *The Economics of Underdevelopment*, eds. A.N. Agarwala and S.P. Singh (London: Oxford University Press, 1958), 189–204, at 190.

[32] Ibid., 190.

[33] See ibid., 191.

[34] Ibid., 190.

[35] Ibid., 190.

[36] Nurkse, *Capital Formation in Underdeveloped Countries*, 156.

"process is better described perhaps as one of assimilation…. [T]o organize a new industry in a less developed country is an art of entrepreneurial initiative. But it is evidently very different from the original process of innovation."[37] This position is a misrepresentation of Schumpeter, He was not concerned with the novelty of technology but how it transformed the economy.

On consumption, Wallich challenged Schumpeter's view that economies were transformed from the generation of new combinations. He argued that unlike in Schumpeter's model, where production takes a central role, "derived development" had to build on consumption. He notes that derived development "is based, not on innovation but on the assimilation of existing innovations. It is this feature that suggests the general concept of derived development—derived from innovations made elsewhere."[38]

This view would lock emerging countries at the tail end of the product cycle, making them perpetual importers of foreign products with no capacity for technological learning. This position reveals Wallich's poor understanding of Schumpeter's view of innovation. The assimilation of imported technology would be consistent with Schumpeter's idea of the creation of new markets, provided this is associated with new combinations.

Other economists offered convenient interpretations of Schumpeter noting that emerging countries lacked the capacity for endogenous growth. Schumpeter argued that economic development comprised such change "as are not forced upon it from without but arise by its own initiative, from within."[39]

Bonné, for example, argued that this view ignores the development impact of "a factory established in an underdeveloped Middle Eastern country by European capital at the height of its flow towards the East half a century ago."[40] For him, such an investment would constitute an imposition from outside and therefore would not be consistent with Schumpeter's view of development. This constitutes a misreading of Schumpeter's concept of economic transformation from within. The example, in fact, fits Schumpeter's view that innovation includes the creation of new markets using existing technologies.

Bonné's contention was that Schumpeter's concept of development was too restrictive to accommodate the needs of emerging regions. Indeed, Schumpeter's theory excluded "mere growth of the economy, as shown by the growth of population and wealth."[41] He focused on the structural transformation of the economy and not merely on expansion in growth.

Bonné pointed out that expansion in population is often a source of innovation. Ironically, he noted that such forces did under certain conditions generate new combinations. He said that the "necessity of expanding production in a densely populated underdeveloped area has, time and again, caused revolutionary changes in local agricultural techniques, and, in particular, in irrigation. Innovation is frequently the result of population pressure, a nexus

---

[37] Wallich, "Some Notes Towards a Theory of Derived Development," 193.

[38] Ibid., 195.

[39] Schumpeter, *The Theory of Economic Development,* 63.

[40] A. Bonné, *Studies in Economic Development: With Special Reference to Conditions in the Underdeveloped Areas of Western Asia and India* (Westport, CT: Greenwood, 1957), 250.

[41] Schumpeter, *The Theory of Economic Development,* 63.

not adequately allowed for in Schumpeter's model."[42]

Bonné maintained that Schumpeter reflected the characteristics of the Western world.[43] Although Schumpeter did not dwell much on the challenges of emerging countries, he offered a universal theory. Schumpeter sought to develop a comprehensive theory of economic sociology as reflected in the "missing Chapter 7" that was excluded from subsequent editions of his book.[44] He thought his theory applied broadly to the "economy, politics, social relations, the arts, science, and morality."[45]

Bonné advanced his own theory that in fact reflected much of Schumpeter's thinking. He defined economic development as consisting of "a series of economic activities causing an increase in the productivity of the economy as a whole and of the individual earner, and also an increase in the ratio of earners to total population."[46] Bonné added new elements such as capital formation, incentives, market expansion, balanced ratio of population increase to economic growth, the use of modern technologies, and political and social regimes conducive to economic development.[47]

His formulation shifted the locus of economic development from endogenous forces at the microeconomic level to wider macroeconomic considerations. It opened up the scope for national planning involving a larger role by state agencies. He noted that since "development in underdeveloped countries is not a self-induced process generated from within, it needs a strong hand to guide and protect it—a function which, at least for a transitional period, will have to be performed by authorities."[48] What was in question was not the role of authorities per se, but how the specific functions that they performed could help to facilitate innovation through the creation of new combinations. To the contrary, he outlined standard bureaucratic functions that were hardly supportive of the dynamic entrepreneurial function for economic development as provided by Schumpeter.

The most comprehensive rejoinder to Wallich was provided by Douglas Rimmer at University College Ghana in 1961. By then, the planning paradigm and the exclusion of alternative approaches to economic development had been firmly established.[49] Rimmer returned to Nurkse's work as the starting point and proceeded to question the basis upon which Wallich rejected the applicability of Schumpeter to emerging countries. He challenged Wallich's view that emerging countries are primarily concerned with consumption.

---

[42] Bonné, *Studies in Economic Development*, 251.

[43] For an assessment of the historical context of Schumpeter's view of entrepreneurship, see A. Ebner, "Schumpeterian Entrepreneurship Revisited: Historical Specificity and the Phases of Capitalist Development," *Journal of the History of Economic Thought* 28 (3) (2006), 314–332.

[44] H. Peukert, "Schumpeter's 'Lost' Seventh Chapter: A Critical Overview," *Industry and Innovation* 9 (1/2) (2002): 79–89; and Y. Shionoya, "The Origin of the Schumpeterian Research Program: A Chapter Omitted from Schumpeter's *Theory of Economic Development*," *Journal of Institutional and Theoretical Economics* 146 (2) (1990), 314–327.

[45] Y. Shionoya, *Schumpeter and the Idea of Social Science* (Cambridge: Cambridge University Press, 1997), 32.

[46] Bonné, *Studies in Economic Development*, 252.

[47] Ibid., 255–256.

[48] Ibid., 258.

[49] See Rimmer, "Schumpeter and the Underdeveloped Countries," 422–450.

He pointed to errors of interpretation such as "identification of innovation with new technology."[50]

Rimmer raised interesting points regarding the impact of short-term pressure to show improvements in economic growth on the extent to which economists were likely to acknowledge the relevance of Schumpeter. This is an important point that downplays long-term investments such as technical training, institution-building, and technological innovation.

In a 1962 response to the decade-long debate, Laumas noted a false dichotomy between investment in infrastructure and improvement in the policy environment. He said that "even though government action in creating infrastructure investment can be conceived to be conducive to the growth of private entrepreneurship, yet it gives rise to the possibility of uncertainties which may tend to vitiate the social climate."[51] He underrated the important role that Schumpeter attached to infrastructure, especially railroads, in fostering entrepreneurship. Laumas also misread Schumpeter's view on the significance of the size of the technological innovation, a common confusion between technical and economic change.[52]

It appears on the surface that Nurske, Wallich, and Bonné shared some common interests in the role of industrial development. But they differ remarkably on the emphasis they place on the role of entrepreneurs. It is also evident from the debates that Schumpeter's critics started with a commitment to the role of planning and did not adequately offer a convincing case on the absence of entrepreneurs in emerging countries. Their focus was on the supremacy of government intervention through government planning processes, paving the way for choosing the state rather than the private sector as the main recipient of development assistance.[53]

Schumpeter's critics carried the day and much of the conduct of development studies continues to stress the role government plays in ways that reduce the private sector's freedom to operate. The influence of Wallich continued to be reflected in scholarly journals well into the 1960s.[54]

Reassessing Hans Singer and the Birth of Development Studies

The rejection of Schumpeter's ideas by development economists was shared widely among leading founders of the field. Probably the most important player in this rejection was Hans Singer, a towering figure in development studies and architect of numerous United Nations (UN) agencies, programs,

---

[50] Ibid., 434.

[51] P.S. Laumas, "Schumpeter's Theory of Economic Development and Underdeveloped Countries," *Quarterly Journal of Economics* 76 (4) (November 1962): 422–450.

[52] For a rebuttal on this topic, see R. Wiles, "Schumpeter and Underdeveloped Countries: Comment," *Quarterly Journal of Economics* 77 (4) (1963): 697–699. As Schumpeter stated, "It should be observed at once that the 'new thing' need not be spectacular or of historical importance. It need not be Bessemer steel or the explosion motor. It can be the Deerfoot sausage." J.A. Schumpeter, "The Creative Response in Economic History," *Journal of Economic History* 7 (2) (November 1947): 151.

[53] L. Mark, "The Favored Status of the State Entrepreneur in Economic Development Programs," *Economic Development and Cultural Change* 7 (4) (1959): 656.

[54] For a rendition of Wallich, see R.C. Wiles, "Professor Joseph Schumpeter and Underdevelopment," *Review of Social Economy* 25 (2) (1967): 196–208.

and projects. Singer's life history to a large extent reflects the debates surrounding Schumpeter's work and that of his contemporaries such as John Maynard Keynes.[55]

It is now acknowledged that Singer was the sole originator of the famous Prebisch-Singer thesis on worsening trade terms between industrialized and developing countries.[56] Singer's 22 years in the United Nations (UN) were devoted to a prodigious career where he contributed immensely to the articulation of new concepts and the creation of international development institutions and programs in fields covering international trade, children, development financing, food aid, science and technology, and development research.[57]

An area that stands out in his work at the UN is his resounding dismissal of the relevance of Schumpeter's ideas to development. He expresses deeply pessimistic views in "Obstacles to Economic Development."[58] From the outset, he argued that Schumpeter's "theory is a good basis for a survey of the general obstacles to economic development, not because it applies to underdeveloped countries but because it fails to apply."[59]

The basis for his analysis is his acceptance of Wallich's three arguments against Schumpeter: the absence of entrepreneurs in those countries and hence the need for government intervention; the lack of capacity to generate new technologies; and the local focus for consumption rather than production. Singer accepted its premises as being consistent with "what can be observed in underdeveloped countries."[60]

Singer argues that the existence of entrepreneurs is not a cause of development but its consequence:

> "From this point of view the Schumpeter system is not really a theory of economic development, in the sense of a theory of how such development starts. Rather, it is a theory of how economic development continues and proceeds, once it has reached a certain stage characterized by the creation of innovating private entrepreneurs, and by the creation of the kind of society in which they can operate."[61]

Singer failed to acknowledge the inspirational model that Schumpeter was using, which was essentially the transformation of the economic system from within. The shift from one economic level to the next was independent of the level at which society was starting off provided there is generation of new combinations, especially in relation to agricultural economies.

Singer, like Wallich, made a strong case for the role of the public sector. He acknowledged, however, the low level of administrative capacity in less-developed

---

[55] There is a separate body of literature that looks at the theoretical and personal differences between Schumpeter and Keynes which will not be reviewed in this paper. Those interested in data on how intellectual history is judging the two might want to look at A.M. Diamond, Jr., "Schumpeter vs. Keynes: 'In the Long Run Not All of Us Are Dead,'" *Journal of the History of Economic Thought* 31 (4) (2009): 531–541. An instructive comparison of the two economists is A. Smithies, "Schumpeter and Keynes," *Review of Economic Statistics* 33 (2) (1951): 163–169.

[56] J. Toye and R. Toye, "The Origins and Interpretation of the Prebisch-Singer Thesis," *History of Political Economy* 35 (3) (2003): 437–467.

[57] Toye, "Hans Singer and International Development," 915–923.

[58] H. Singer, "Obstacles to Economic Development," *Social Research* 19 (4) (1953): 19–31.

[59] Ibid. 19.

[60] Ibid., 19.

[61] Ibid., 23.

countries, and—like Schumpeter in the case of entrepreneurs—stressed the quality of human resources. Singer's case for improving "public administration" could have been made for "business administration" as well. By then, technical assistance programs were being developed through new international development agencies.[62] This was not the case everywhere, however. For example, the development of the semiconductor industry in Taiwan benefited from U.S. technical assistance programs that involved combinations of private and public sector players.[63]

Working from the theories of factor endowment and product cycle, Singer rejected Schumpeter's idea of endogenous innovation and argued for a "technology transfer" model consistent with the concept of "derived development" as put forward by Wallich. He did not think that modern technologies developed for industrialized-country consumers were appropriate for less-developed countries. His view clearly misrepresented Schumpeter by focusing on new technologies rather than on new economic structures.

In addition, Singer's prognosis was particularly gloomy. He argued that "a different technology, and in many ways an older or 'inferior' one, would be more appropriate….In many respects the technology of a hundred years ago would be desirable for them, and would make their economic development easier."[64] To compound this pessimistic view, he said "that technology no longer exists. It has been scrapped, and rightly scrapped, in the industrialized coun-tries—and the technology of the industrialized countries is the only existing technology."[65] He added that "[u]p to a point, it may have been an advantage to be a latecomer in economic development, but by now it has clearly turned into a serious disadvantage."[66]

Wallich and Singer put excessive faith in the goodwill of governments. They assumed that government officials would naturally respond to democratic pressure to increase the living conditions of the people.[67] But in many cases the state has been abused for personal gain. Many of the East Asian countries that have strived to improve the economic conditions of the people cannot attribute their motivations solely to democratic pressure.

Singer was a prominent development thinker and the extent to which his views influenced development practice is a subject for further enquiry. What is evident is that his thinking was congruent with the conduct of international development agencies and remains so currently, despite the rise of ideas such as "private–public partnerships." He and other critics of the relevance of Schumpeter not only failed to appreciate the importance of entrepreneurship in development, but they took a view of the role of government that in the end could not achieve the same transformational changes they wanted.

Singer would later return to the issue of science and technology but through his view that technology played a role in the prevalence of the "dual economy" and efforts were needed to facilitate its trans-

---

[62] Staples, *The Birth of Development*.

[63] C-Y. Hung, et al. "Global Industrial Migration: The Case of the Integrated Circuit Industry," *International Journal of Technology and Globalisation* 2 (3–4) (2006): 362–376.

[64] Ibid., 25.

[65] Ibid., 25.

[66] Ibid., 26.

[67] Ibid., 30.

fer to developing countries. This view is indeed consistent with the "derived development" concept that Wallich used as a basis for rejecting Schumpeter's relevance to emerging countries. Singer, however, understood that the successful transfer of "appropriate technologies" would require a functional domestic infrastructure.[68]

Christopher Freeman, who created the Science Policy Research Unit at the University of Sussex, agreed with Singer, and their joint work resulted in the creation of the "Sussex Group," which Singer chaired. In 1970, it produced a highly influential document, *The Sussex Manifesto: Science and Technology to Developing Countries during the Second Development Decade*, which was incorporated into UN documents and became a basis for subsequent international decisions on technology transfer.[69]

These efforts led to the Vienna 1979 UN Conference on Science and Technology for Development, which created a commission, fund, and center to implement its decisions.[70] The "technology transfer" debate quickly became highly acrimonious as it extended to cover issues such as intellectual property. The diplomatic push for "technology transfer" was seen by Singer as a way to correct the global economy duopoly and very much mirrored the overall imbalance in trade relations. But industrialized countries saw it as impinging on the intellectual property rights that were owned not by governments but by enterprises. Ironically, this program that put power in the hands of governments and largely excluded the private sector did not face new pressures to protect private sector interests.

In 1993, the UN Centre for Science and Technology for Development was abolished. The UN Fund on Science and Technology for Development was absorbed by the UN Development Programme. Only the UN Commission for Science and Technology for Development survived the purge and was integrated into the UN Conference on Trade and Development. The UN created a variety of science and technology advisory mechanisms, but they were hardly effective, partly because they were providing advice that nobody asked for or acted on when provided.[71]

Recasting Schumpter: Policy Implications

Schumpeter's prescient ideas laid a firm basis upon which researchers and policymakers are now reshaping development policies in the context of innovation.

---

[68] See H.W. Singer, "Dualism Revisited: A New Approach to the Problems of the Dual Society in Developing Countries," *Journal of Development Studies* 7 (1) (October 1970): 63. It is notable that Singer uses the word "appropriate technology." This is not accidental. According to D.J. Shaw, "He admired the work of E.F. Schumacher, the chairman of the Intermediate Technology Development Group in London, who first introduced the concept of 'intermediate technology' in a report for the Indian Planning Commission in 1963. Schumacher emphasized that 'small is beautiful' and stressed the importance of smaller-scale, labour-intensive, and the more natural or organic, technologies developed for Third World countries." Shaw, *Sir Hans Singer*, 177–178

[69] The Sussex Group helped to prepare a "World Plan of Action on the Application of Science and Technology to Development" for the United Nations. Ibid., 174–179.

[70] National Academy of Sciences, *Knowledge and Diplomacy: Science Advice in the United Nations System* (Washington, D.C.: National Academy of Sciences, 2002), 6–11.

[71] G. Oldham, "Science and Technology Advice within the United Nations: Some Lessons from Past Experience," *Science and Public Policy* 33 (9) (2006): 647–651.

As Fagerberg rightly notes, "Students of long-run economic change used to focus on factors such as capital accumulation or the working of markets, rather than on innovation. This is now changing. Research on the role of innovation in economic and social change has proliferated in recent years…and with a bent towards cross-disciplinarity."[72]

The most elaborate international effort to bring Schumpeterian ideas to bear on development efforts is the Global Network for Economics of Learning, Innovation, and Competence Building Systems (Globelics), which held its first conference in Denmark in 2002. Since then Globelics conferences have been held on nearly all continents, and the first Globelics Academy was convened in Lisbon in 2005. More than 2,000 scholars have participated in Globelics conferences and over 300 doctoral students have been part of the Globelics Academy. Regional Globelics chapters are being created around the world to foster interactions between researchers and policymakers.

In seeking to recast Schumpeter to reflect contemporary economic decision-making, it is important to spell out a few key elements of his thinking that enjoy universal appeal. These critical elements should have been the basis upon which to genuinely assess the relevance of his ideas for emerging countries. The most important limitation of many of Schumpeter's critics is that they failed to review his work in its totality but instead tendentiously selected ideas that could be debated outside his overall conceptual framework.

Innovation as creative destruction

Schumpeter's relevance to emerging countries is his disruptive model that provided the basis for his theory of economic development. Neither entrepreneurs nor markets can function without the existence of basic infrastructure that allows them to produce and transport goods. But building such infrastructure disrupts the existing economic system.

Schumpeter's disruptive model was railroads, a key infrastructure that had profoundly transformed the world he studied.[73] For Schumpeter, railroads were not just a source of economic development per se, but a driving force in improving human welfare, ironically in the same way as advocated by his critics: "While a new thing is being built and financed, expenditure is on a supernormal level, and through a normal state of incomes we get all those symptoms which we associate with prosperity."[74]

Railroad expansion did not involve creating new technologies but deploying existing ones. In Schumpeter's view, "getting things done" was "pure entrepreneurship stripped of all accessories."[75] It involved the "leadership of groups, in successfully dealing with politicians and local interests, in the solution of problems of management and of development in the regions of the roads opened up."[76] The entrepreneurial function was performed by either individuals or groups of people whose tasks were unrelated to the act of taking financial risks.

---

[72] J. Fagerberg, "Innovation: A Guide to the Literature," in Fagerberg, D. Mowery, and R. Nelson, *The Oxford Handbook of Innovation*, eds. J. Fagerberg, D. Mowery, and R. Nelson, (Oxford: Oxford University Press, 2005), 1.

[73] Schumpeter, *Business Cycles*, 304.

[74] J.A. Schumpeter, "An Economic Interpretation of Our Time: The Lowell Lectures," in The Economics and Sociology of Capitalism, ed., Richard Swedberg (Princeton, NJ: Princeton University Press, 1941), 347-349.

[75] Schumpeter, "The Meaning of Rationality in the Social Sciences," in Swedberg, *The Economics and Sociology of Capitalism*, 327.

[76] Ibid., 327.

In fact, Schumpeter contended that it was funders, not entrepreneurs, who took financial risks, as evidenced by the emergence of innovations in credit-providing institutions and other approaches for underwriting the risks such as state enterprises.

Critics of the application of the Schumpeterian model to emerging economies pointed out that these countries are often dominated by peasant farming, which in their view is not entrepreneurial because farmers tend to be perceived largely as producers whose output is then processed elsewhere. By their very nature, however, farmers are engaged in the constant creation of new combinations that involve discontinuous adaptations. Like in many industries they engage in routine practices that use established methods. But there are frequent occasions when farmers are forced to creatively respond to changes in their conditions. Under those circumstances their behavior is hardly different from that of entrepreneurs in other sectors.[77]

Over the centuries, agriculture has shown remarkable capacity for entrepreneurial activity where key foundations for economic transformation and critical support systems such as research and development, infrastructure, technical training, credit, and improved policy environment are available to farmers. The great agricultural transformations of the last 150 years occurred in the United States, India, Brazil, China, and Mexico, among others, and resulted from efforts to increase foundations and support systems upon which entrepreneurship thrives. It is precisely the absence of these types of investments and the application of "derived development" models in the form of food aid that largely explain the low level of entrepreneurship in African agriculture. It is not just the years of neglect that affected African agriculture.[78]

It is therefore notable that these foundations were also the only ones that received little policy attention in the "derived development" model. The challenges of emerging countries were compounded by international trade policies that punished them with tariff escalation if they tried to add value to their exports. In effect, they were structurally discouraged from creating new combinations.

Schumpeter's example of railroads has two important policy implications for the current discourse of innovation policy. First, it underscores the importance of physical infrastructure in emerging countries. Such infrastructure, and the associated institutional changes, creates opportunities for entrepreneurs not only to participate in its construction but also to expand opportunities for new businesses. Second, infrastructure transforms the economic system in a discontinuous way by not only disrupting previous economic practices, but also by expanding opportunities for new economic combinations. Infrastructure projects serve as centers of origin and diffusion of technical capabilities into the wider economy. It is these same radical transformations that Schumpeter's critics wished to see in emerging countries but rejected the approaches that would have allowed for their advancement.

---

[77] These dual attributes of farmers are discussed in R.E. Sachs, "The Farmer—An Entrepreneurial Personality? A Socio-Psychological Analysis of Decision-Making, with Special Regard to the Economic Behaviour of Farmers," *Sociologia Ruralis* 13 (2) (1973): 195–214; and M. Niska, H. Vesala, and K. Vesala, "Peasantry and Entrepreneurship as Frames for Farming: Reflections on Farmers' Values and Agricultural Policy Discourses," *Sociologia Ruralis* 52 (4) (2012): 453–469.

[78] This theme is explored in detail in C. Juma, *The New Harvest: Agricultural Innovation in Africa* (New York: Oxford University Press, 2011).

We return to the importance of system-wide technological and economic discontinuities. Schumpeter foresaw and articulated clearly the political and social implications of such discontinuity in his later works, especially *Business Cycles* and *Capitalism, Socialism and Democracy*—very much in the spirit of the systems approach that he first sketched out in the "missing Chapter 7." Schumpeter's idea of "creative destruction" has its roots in the very nature of capitalism.[79]

The disruptive nature of these events is evident and consistent with the logic of endogenous and system-wide discontinuous change. These changes are not driven by demand, but instead are "forced by producers on consumers."[80]

A broader societal view brings up additional policy concerns such as the welfare impacts of "the gales of creative destruction,"[81] that have been expressed in the form of organized resistance to new technologies. A contemporary example of this phenomenon is the global debate on the adoption of transgenic crops.[82]

Human Capabilities

An equally important source of system-wide disruptive force arising from Schumpeter's theory is the role of human capabilities. The various tasks that Schumpeter ascribes to the entrepreneur cannot be performed without paying special attention to this role. Similarly, the illustrative case of railroads was an example of the importance of technical competence. Such capabilities are equally needed where society is simply adapting to change. But according to Schumpeter, human capabilities are even more critical when a society is engaged in creative economic responses.[83]

To Schumpeter, the quality of human resources was critical to the execution of the entrepreneurial function. Models of "derived development" would not appreciate the significance of building capacity in emerging countries. Indeed, when they did, the emphasis was on building up a cadre of functionaries for the public service. Technical fields such as science, technology, and engineering were largely considered irrelevant to emerging countries except in limited areas where they supported assimilation of imported products or inevitable areas of adaptive research such as plant breeding. Even more critical was the low priority given to higher education in general and higher technical education in particular.

The three areas raised here—systems approaches to economic development; inspirational and practical roles of infrastructure investments in development; and the role of human capabilities—were evident challenges in the early phases of development studies.

---

[79] Schumpeter, *Capitalism, Socialism and Democracy*, 83.

[80] Schumpeter, *Business Cycles*, 73.

[81] C. Schubert, "How to Evaluate Creative Destruction: Reconstructing Schumpeter's Approach," *Cambridge Journal of Economics* 37 (2) (March 2013): 227–250, at 229; and C. Schubert, "Is Novelty Always a Good Thing? Towards an Evolutionary Welfare Economics," *Journal of Evolutionary Economics* 22, 3 (2012): 585–619.

[82] On the political juxtaposition of activists vs. corporations, see, for example, R. Schurman and W. Munro, *Fighting for the Future of Food: Activists versus Agribusiness* (Minneapolis: University of Minnesota Press, 2010). For an evolutionary interpretation of resistance to innovation, see J. Mokyr, "Technological Inertia in Economic History," *The Journal of Economic History* 52 (2) (1992): 325–338; and J. Mokyr, "Punctuated Equilibria and Technological Progress," *American Economic Review* 80 (2) (1990): 350–354.

[83] Schumpeter, "The Creative Response in Economic History," 150.

Schumpeter offered a superior starting point for thinking about development. However, the preoccupation with planning, which is a narrow function of the state, resulted in the rejection of important ideas that would later help to drive East Asian economies. Japan, which adopted a different approach to economic recovery, demonstrated congruence with Schumpeter's ideas.[84]

One key aspect of building technological capabilities is the growing interest among developing countries to use existing technologies but to pursue alternative development pathways. To some extent this is driven by the desire to break out from some of the technological paradigms that have come with a wide range of social and ecological costs.

Role of Government

Schumpeter displayed a fascinating lack of interest in discussing the policy implications of his work. Schumpeter's understanding of the place of government in his theory of development is particularly important in light of efforts by his critics to view government as a substitute for the entrepreneur.

Schumpeter viewed the role of the state as belonging to the wider context of system-wide "economic sociology" and subject to the same principles covering the creation of new combinations. He avoided the deterministic discussion on the relationships between economic and political actors.

In fact, "economic sociology" dealt largely with "economically relevant institutions, including habits and all forms of behavior in general, such as government, property, private enterprise, customary, or 'rational' behavior."[85]

Economic sociology gave Schumpeter the opportunity to explore institutional innovations that accompany technological change and economic transformation. These innovations are driven by internal interests that may or may not align with entrepreneurial activities in the private sector.[86] In addition, Schumpeter was acutely aware of institutional persistence: "Social structures, types and attitudes are coins that do not readily melt. Once they are formed they persist, possibly for centuries..."[87] The implications of institutional persistence for development are quite evident but were not the subject of much intellectual interest among Schumpeter's critics.[88]

The fundamental implication of Schumpeter's view is that government institutions have their own evolutionary dynamics that may not necessarily align with development objectives. Moreover, when established, such institutions are self-replicating. Many of the structural reform programs promoted by the World Bank and the International Monetary Fund in emerging countries were aimed at dealing with the issue of institutional persistence.

The real question, however, is not so much about substituting government for the entrepreneur. It is about finding ways

---

[84] T.K. McCraw, "Schumpeter Ascending," *American Scholar* 60 (3) (1991): 371–392.

[85] J.A. Schumpeter, "The Communist Manifesto in Sociology and Economics," *Journal of Political Economy* 57 (3) (June 1949): 203–204.

[86] A. Ebner, "Institutions, Entrepreneurship, and the Rationale of Government: An Outline of the Schumpeterian Theory of the State," *Journal of Economic Behavior and Organization* 59 (4) (2006): 497–515.

[87] Schumpeter, *Capitalism, Socialism and Democracy*, 12.

[88] For example, despite being acknowledged as important, the issue is relegated to an appendix in Bonné, *Studies in Economic Development*, 261–271.

in which the state could perform entrepreneurial functions either in its own right or in support of the private sector or some combination thereof. In other words, recognizing the importance of innovation in economic development requires a broader view of the sources of entrepreneurship beyond the private sector. Assigning the state an entrepreneurial role would resolve the false dichotomy sketched out by Wallich and his supporters.

In examining the emergence of the entrepreneurial state in East Asian economies, Ebner has noted key functions that include identification of emerging techno-economic paradigms; creating open economies that are part of global competitiveness strategies; formation of entrepreneurial capacity; promotion of knowledge flows among actors in national innovation systems; and creation of conditions that support business incubation and scale-up.[89]

The rising focus on innovation for economic development creates opportunities for emerging countries to revisit the work of Schumpeter.[90] Unlike their predecessors who had to contend with a limited reading of Schumpeter's work, emerging countries have a much larger pool of knowledge to draw upon. First, they have access to Schumpeter's prescient works, thanks to advances in technology. Second, they have access to experiences arising from the earlier applications of Schumpeter's work. Third, and more important, there is a growing body of neo-Schumpeterian scholarship that offers an untapped reservoir of ideas that can be adapted to their contemporary needs.[91]

Getting the state to perform these entrepreneurial functions requires a better understanding of the systemic nature of the public policy process.[92] It entails a level of institutional orchestration that cannot be achieved through simplistic notions such as correction of market failures. Taking this approach will also involve developing new policy instruments that reflect the structure and functions of innovation systems.[93] As emerging economies increasingly recognize that fostering innovation requires significantly different approaches, they might just become the flag bearers of policy approaches inspired by Schumpeter over a century ago.

Conclusion

The aim of this paper is to explore the rejection of Schumpeter's ideas by the founders of development economics. Contrary to popular perceptions, the absence of Schumpeter in contemporary development policy discourse is not a historical oversight. It is a result of nearly a decade of debate starting in the 1950s. The debate

---

[89] A. Ebner, "Public Policy, Governance and Innovation: Entrepreneurial States in East Asian Economic Development," *International Journal of Technology and Globalisation* 3 (1) (2007): 117–118.

[90] J. Fagerberg and K. Sapprasert, "National Innovation Systems: The Emergence of a New Approach," *Science and Public Policy* 38 (9) (2011): 669–679.

[91] See, for example, Bengt-Åke Lundvall et al., eds., *Handbook of Innovation Systems and Developing Countries* (Cheltenham, UK: Edward Edgar, 2009). See also D. Hartmann et al., "Applying Comprehensive Neo-Schumpeterian Economics to Latin American Economies," *Structural Change and Economic Dynamics* 21 (1) (2010): 70–83.

[92] E. Ramstad, "Expanding Innovation Systems and Policy: An Organisational Perspective," *Policy Studies* 30 (5) (2009): 533–553.

[93] A. Wieczorek and M. Hekkert, "Systemic Instruments for Systemic Innovation Problems: A Framework for Policy Makers and Innovation Scholars," *Science and Public Policy* 39 (1) (2012): 74–87.

represented a clash between Schumpeter's systems approach to economic development and dominant equilibrium theories that dominated economic thought. Schumpeter's detractors institutionalized their theories in various international organizations, especially the United Nations, the World Bank, and the International Monetary Fund. They were therefore able to lock in their ideas in ways that made Schumpeterian creative destruction a long and tedious process.

Schumpeter laid out the foundations for understanding how economies change over time. That was a century ago. Several enduring themes of his theory remain valid today and should be part of the core of the policies of emerging nations. First, priority should be given to the role of innovation not only in transforming economic systems to new levels of performance, but also in spreading prosperity. Second, emphasis should be placed on the role of entrepreneurs in the private and public sectors as critical agents of innovation. Third, reducing all types of risks associated with innovation should be a central feature of economic governance. Finally, private entrepreneurs and public servants should undertake important but complementary leadership roles. Elaborating on these themes and adjusting them to reflect contemporary circumstances will help to advance our understanding and management of economies as complex systems.

Policy and Complex Systems - Volume 1 Issue 1 - Spring 2014

Realizing Complex Policy: Using a Systems-of-Systems Approach to Develop and Implement Policy

Dr. David H Dombkins

Contents:

1. Executive Summary

Sustainable Development[1], along with changes to the global economic model, are examples of Complex Policies that cannot be realized using traditional approaches to policy formulation and implementation.

Rather than focusing on WHAT is to be the final content of policies such as the United Nations Sustainable Development Goals (SDGs), this paper provides a robust methodology for HOW governments can design, implement, deliver, and manage policies and action plans to realize complex policies.

While traditional approaches to policy have been effective in the past, there is a growing international recognition that traditional approaches to policy formulation and realization are not suited to the systemic and highly complex issues facing our world and our societies.[2]

The paper defines three distinct policy strategies—Bespoke, Evolutionary, and Emergent—and provides a tool for categorization of policies. Each policy strategy has a range of applications dependent upon its complexity and uncertainty (Refer to Figure 1).

The paper's focus is on providing governments with reliable strategies and methodologies to design and realize complex policies such as the SDGs and Sustainable Economic Development.

In implementing complex policy such as the SDGs, governments will have a range of policy strategy, design, and im-

---

[1] Sustainable Development Goals (SDG) should be action oriented, concise, easy to communicate, limited in number, aspirational at the global level, universally applicable taking into account national realities, capacities, and levels of development.

[2] J. Chapman, *System Failure: Why Governments must Learn to Think Differently*. Demos, 2004..
System Stewardship. The UK Institute of Government, 2011.
E. Lindquist, *Grappling with Complex Policy Challenges* (Australian National University, HC Coombs Policy Forum, 2011).

To view the electronic version of this journal and this image, scan the code below or visit: http://www.ipsonet.org/publications/open-access/policy-and-complex-systems/ volume-1-number-1-spring-2014

Figure 1. Three Types of Policies

plementation options. While some of these policies will be easily defined and can be implemented using traditional approaches, other policies will be very complex and need to be implemented using approaches suited to complexity.

As shown in Figure 2, through categorizing policies (and their components) into one of the three types (Bespoke, Evolutionary, or Emergent), governments can better plan the policy design, implementation, and management strategies.

The paper brings together theory and practice from public policy, complexity, and innovative work from the U.S. and Australian Departments of Defense in the design and management of complexity. Many of the terms and language used in this paper draw from these disciplines and experience.

This paper provides a valuable foundation for governments and researchers to develop the strategies, methodologies, and capabilities necessary to develop strategies and action plans for successfully realizing complex policies.

2. Introduction

The quality of life enjoyed by citizens globally, both now and into the future, is dependent upon the success of today's policies addressing complex issues in sustainability, poverty, health, economic development, defense, infrastructure, energy, education, etc. These complex world policy issues cannot be resolved by using the traditional strategy for policy design and implementation. Neither can they be resolved through attempting to use a Design School[3] approach in designing and implementing meta-policies that attempt to integrate multiple component policies.

Policies to realize the complex issues, such as SDGs, will be difficult to design and plan, as the issues facing the world are complex and are affected by ongoing social, political, financial, and technical change and emergence. Adding to this complexity will be the need to deliver the SDGs through multiple agents where the SDG owner often does not have directive control over the agents. Traditional management methodologies, where planning is completed by experts and then sequentially implemented and delivered, are inappropriate for complex policies.

The paper presents strategies and methodologies for the design, implementation, delivery, and emergent management of complex policies. The development of strategies and methodologies for the management of complexity has been a pivotal issue in defense, where asymmetric warfare and network-centric warfare are complex endeavors that cannot be designed, planned, implemented, and operated using traditional project management strategies and methodologies.

Complex policy, as with complex programs, are non-linear and recursive, and do not reflect the sequential planning of the traditional approach. This complexity is particularly evident in defense where complex programs operate as systems-of-systems within an emergent environment.

The United States Office of the Secretary of Defense (U.S., OSD) Systems Engineering Guide[4] for systems-of-systems uses a recursive and non-linear Trapeze model (refer Figure 3) with seven core elements as a mechanism to understand the behavior of complex systems.

While the Trapeze Model is a useful construct, it is not easily understood or

---

[3] M. Porter, *Competitive Strategy: Techniques for Analysing Industries and Competitors* (New York: Free Press, 1980).

To view the electronic version of this journal and this image, scan the code below or visit:
http://www.ipsonet.org/publications/open-access/policy-and-complex-systems/
volume-1-number-1-spring-2014

Figure 2. Overview of Policy Strategy Options

To view the electronic version of this journal and this image, scan the code below or visit:
http://www.ipsonet.org/publications/open-access/policy-and-complex-systems/
volume-1-number-1-spring-2014

Figure 3. U.S. Trapeze Model

useful in designing and managing complex systems or policies.

The WAVE Planning Model[5] (refer Figure 4) has been used as a mechanism for reconfiguring the Trapeze model as an intuitive series of major implementation steps.

WAVE Planning has enabled modeling and sensemaking using the agent-based life cycle modeling[6], and alternative strategies to be analyzed for value sustainment in systems-of-systems.[7]

The U.S. OSD approach to systems-of-systems purposefully does not deal with the decision-making process necessary to establish and support a systems-of-systems. In complex policies, the policymaking process is itself complex and is integral to the policy's design, implementation, and ongoing management.

The U.S. OSD Wave Plan Model[8] provides a core process model for architectural design, simulation, implementation, and ongoing management of emergence for complex policies. However, the number of core elements and overall complexity of the model are significantly increased through both the introduction of pluralism into the system, and the change in focus from a Directed to Collaborative and sometimes Virtual systems-of-systems.

Figure 5 shows the Complex Policy Model for complex policy design, implementation, delivery, and emergent ongoing management.

As with the U.S. OSD Trapeze model, when converted to a WAVE Plan and integrated with the systems-of-systems WAVE Plan, the resultant WAVE Plan is intuitive, readily understood, and can be used to plan and manage complex policies (Refer to Figures 6 and 7).

The Wave Plan for Complex Policy has two components, each of which is a systems-of-systems in their own right:

- Policy objectives, strategy, and political support
- Policy emergent implementation, using systems-of-systems.

These two component systems operate at different rhythms and with very different rule sets. The WAVE Plan for Complex Policy enables these two separate component systems-of-systems to operate as a Meta-systems-of-systems, and for them to be jointly planned and managed.

[4] US Office of the Secretary of Defense, *Systems Engineering Guide for Systems of Systems.* Version 1.0, August, 2008.

[5] D. Dombkins, "Project Managed Change: the Application of Project Management Techniques to Strategic Change Programs." Centre for Corporate Change Working Paper No. 062, Australian Graduate School of Management, The University of New South Wales, 1996.

[6] P. Acheson, L. Pape, G. Dagli, N. Kilican-Ergin, J. Columbi, and K. Haris, "Understanding Systems-of-Systems Using an Agent-Based Wave Model," in *Complex Adaptive Systems*, Publication 2, Editor in Chief Cihan H. Dagli, Conference Organized by Missouri University of Science and Technology 2012, Washington DC, 2012.

[7] N. Ricci, A. Ross, D. Rhodes, and M. Fitzgerald, "Considering Alternative Strategies for Value Sustainment in Systems-of-Systems." SEAri Working Paper Series, WP-2012-3-2. Systems Engineering Advancement Research Initiative, Massachusetts Institute of Technology, Cambridge, 2013.

[8] J. Dahmann, J. Lane, R. Lowry, and K. Baldwin, "An Implementers View of Systems Engineering for Systems-of-systems." IEEE International Systems Conference, Montreal, Canada, April, 2011.

To view the electronic version of this journal and this image, scan the code below or visit:
http://www.ipsonet.org/publications/open-access/policy-and-complex-systems/
volume-1-number-1-spring-2014

Figure 4. SoS WAVE Plan Complex Policy Model

To view the electronic version of this journal and this image, scan the code below or visit:
http://www.ipsonet.org/publications/open-access/policy-and-complex-systems/
volume-1-number-1-spring-2014

Figure 5. Complex Policy Model

To view the electronic version of this journal and this image, scan the code below or visit:
http://www.ipsonet.org/publications/open-access/policy-and-complex-systems/
volume-1-number-1-spring-2014

Figure 6. Complex Policy Model converted to WAVE Plan

To view the electronic version of this journal and this image, scan the code below or visit:
http://www.ipsonet.org/publications/open-access/policy-and-complex-systems/
volume-1-number-1-spring-2014

Figure 7. Complex Policy WAVE Plan

3. Policy for a Complex World: A Journey

*I*s the policy so complex that it is better for the agents to address it through adaptation, rather than through the policy owner trying to specify a solution in advance?

The realization of complex policies is best viewed as a non-linear and recursive journey, with Process Governance, WAVE Planning, and Stewardship employed to help manage the emergent journey.

Complex policies are often unfamiliar and emergent, and there is often little agreement on what the policy should look like, let alone how the policy can or should be realized (in areas as diverse as sustainability, crime, employment, public health, energy security, etc.).

From a risk management perspective, there is a strong case for letting the multiple agents within the adaptive systems-of-systems handle the complexity, rather than policyowners trying to specify a specific solution in advance.

Policyowners are more effective in setting high-level goals and delivery solutions that can be progressively adapted to an emergent policy environment. For example, technically-oriented policies are generally better implemented by using new technologies strategically and leveraging-off legacy systems, rather than implementing a full replacement of all legacy technologies. Through using an emergent strategy, policyowners can assess the effectiveness of the inserted technology, and then progressively review new technologies for insertion.

Ongoing achievements in science, medicine, and engineering have created high expectations within the broader community as to the effectiveness of reductionist strategies. While the scientific method is very effective in many areas, its reductionist and deductive-based approaches are notably unsuccessful in designing and implementing complex policies.

A major contemporary risk to policyowners is that individuals and organizations will behave asymmetrically in response to policy and laws so as to avoid and/or reduce the effect of policies and laws. Commercial businesses and professional advisers have made an art of manipulating the wording used in laws and policies in order to avoid or distort their intent.

In our complex world, the most effective policies and laws define high level outcomes that are difficult to misinterpret or distort, and that establish a process where the detailed operation of the policy is progressively changed to counteract any asymmetric behaviors used to circumvent the intent of the policy.

It is difficult to standardize complex policy outcome, due to the high level of emergence; the policyowners' lack of directive control over implementation; and multiple delivery agents. Complex policy is not simply formulated and then executed (Refer to Figure 8). it is designed and constantly re-designed by multiple players throughout the system, as many multiple agents working together within the systems-of-systems adapt the policy's outcomes.

Therefore policyowners need to:

- design complex policies with high-level goals that are resilient to the level of emergence that is likely to occur; and
- establish a governance system:
  - where the implementation and delivery strategy is purposefully designed to take a major role in shaping the policy over its lifecycle; and
  - to oversee the ways in which the policy is being adapted by the multi-

To view the electronic version of this journal and this image, scan the code below or visit:
http://www.ipsonet.org/publications/open-access/policy-and-complex-systems/
volume-1-number-1-spring-2014

Figure 8. Complex policies are very difficult, if not impossible, to fully design in advance

To view the electronic version of this journal and this image, scan the code below or visit:
http://www.ipsonet.org/publications/open-access/policy-and-complex-systems/
volume-1-number-1-spring-2014

Figure 9. PCAT defines strategy

ple agents, and that enables the policyowner to steer the systems-of-systems toward the policyowner's high-level goals.

Given the need for flexibility of policy systems, effective decision making needs to adapt as new information becomes available—and much of that information will come from the process of decision making itself. Therefore, those implementing and delivering a policy need to have authority devolved to provide them with the capacity and opportunity to adapt it to local or changing circumstances. Thus, governance involves policyowners devolving responsibility for local implementation and delivery to agents, overseeing how the policy is being adapted, and attempting to steer the system if it is deviating too far away from the policy's high-level goals.

Depending upon the degree of control the policyowner has over the agents, different governance processes are required:

- Directive: Where the policyowner has directive control over the agents, a governance system developed for defense programs called Integrated Process and Product Development (IPPD) can be adapted. The IPPD system establishes a formal governance structure and integrated operational teams.
- Participative/Consultative: Where the policyowner does not have directive control over the agents, the policyowner must rely on establishing a cooperative/participative based governance system. The Process Governance system developed for complex programs provides a proven governance system. Process Governance includes a process system that manages emergence, and incorporates both Partnering and the Integrated Teams component of IPPD.

Regardless of the governance system used, the policyowner needs to establish a suitable strategy and capability for policy journey management (design, implementation, delivery, and emergence).

Research into complex policies has found that:

- Complex policies operate as networks, are not able to be decomposed into basic elements, are not able to be predicted, and are emergent.
- Policy formulation and implementation are not separate, but intrinsically linked.
- The potential outcomes of the policy itself may change significantly during implementation.
- Complex policies involve multiple stakeholders and agents that the policyowner cannot directly control.
- Asymmetric behaviors are used by those impacted by policies to avoid, mitigate, or distort the intent of the policy.
- The outcomes of complex policies are often adapted as they are realized in practice. Complex policies are not just formulated and then executed; they are designed and constantly re-designed by the multiple players interacting within a systems-of-systems environment.

Policies vary in their level of predictability. Therefore, different strategies and methodologies are required for different types of policies. The paper provides three different strategies (Bespoke, Evolutionary, and Emergent) to consider in policy design, implementation, and delivery.

Bespoke

The bespoke strategy is suited to policy areas where the policy can be fully designed and planned in advance, and when a centralized and directive control system can effectively supervise the policy's implementation and delivery. The bespoke strategy uses an evidence-based deductive approach in policy design, and a linear, centralized, and directive approach in planning for implementation and delivery of policies (Refer to Figure 10).

The bespoke strategy defines specific goals and develops detailed implementation plans, in a manner similar to the engineering design process used for infrastructure construction. In the same way that engineers use specific plans to manage the delivery of infrastructure, governments use bespoke strategies as levers to drive change in society.

Key to the bespoke strategy is the capability of the design process to turn the government's brief into highly detailed and integrated plans and specifications. The bespoke strategy is dependent upon the accuracy of the design and the implementation and delivery strategy to deliver a fully operational service from 'day one'.

Traditional project management and systems engineering provide reliable tools and processes for the implementation and delivery of detailed bespoke policies.

Policies can fail when the wrong strategy is selected. For example, policies that have a high reliance on technology or software applications are suited to emergent policy strategies that enable technical risks and service delivery models to be resolved before a broad rollout of the policy.

Evolutionary

An evolutionary strategy is based upon the same processes that are used by the bespoke strategy, applying them sequentially to progressively refine and build the capability of the policy. The evolutionary strategy is suited to complicated policies that require the integration of multiple bespoke policies.

There are two types of evolutionary strategy:

Staged Evolutionary Strategy: As shown in Figure 11, the staged evolutionary strategy allows for an initial version of the policy to be released (providing a limited policy scope), with subsequent iteration of the policy delivering greater policy scope.

The staged evolutionary strategy uses pilot projects and a staged rollout of the policy—for example, the establishment of a central agency for social services that brings together multiple component policy areas into a one-stop shop. The policy implementation risks are greatly reduced through using a staged evolutionary strategy to merge and integrate the multiple services.

Refinement Evolutionary Strategy: In the refinement strategy, an initial policy design and realization plan are completed, and then progressively refined through a series of reviews and development cycles. This strategy is focused on decreasing uncertainty and increasing integration prior to the policy's implementation and delivery.

A refinement evolutionary strategy is very effective in progressively introducing more levels of detail and issues into a policy. However, the effectiveness of this strategy is dependent upon the rigor of the design management process.

To view the electronic version of this journal and this image, scan the code below or visit:
http://www.ipsonet.org/publications/open-access/policy-and-complex-systems/
volume-1-number-1-spring-2014

Figure 10. Linear Planning process for Bespoke Strategy

To view the electronic version of this journal and this image, scan the code below or visit:
http://www.ipsonet.org/publications/open-access/policy-and-complex-systems/
volume-1-number-1-spring-2014

Figure 11. Staged Evolutionary Strategy

To view the electronic version of this journal and these images, scan the code below or visit:
http://www.ipsonet.org/publications/open-access/policy-and-complex-systems/
volume-1-number-1-spring-2014

Figure 12. Refinement Evolutionary Strategy

Figure 13. The Design Process

Figure 13 shows how the design process goes vertically from concept to detail, that is, from very broad issues such as design philosophy in the concept phase, down to the fine definition of project details. In moving from concept to detailed design, the design process follows a cyclic process, cycling between divergent abstract ideas, then through convergent concrete realization, back through abstract ideas, and so on.

Milestone review points facilitate this divergent and convergent thinking process—divergent thinking focus allows for innovation and creativity, and convergent thinking allows the mind to make and integrate as many connections as possible.

Milestone review points are crucial in managing the design process when there are multiple parties involved. The individual designers are re-benchmarked at each milestone review point, so that all the designers then proceed to the next part of the design from the same position. After the milestone point, the individual designers will again diverge, but will be re-benchmarked again at the next milestone point.

Emergent

Policies that need to bring multiple systems together to deliver a higher order outcome, or that are subject to ongoing frame-breaking change in underpinning aspects, are subject to emergent behavior. Emergent behaviors appear when the components of the policy interact to deliver unpredictable outcomes. These unpredictable outcomes can be both beneficial and detrimental to the policy.

Some complex policies operate as complex adaptive systems that can be pushed out of balance even to the point of collapse through negatively reinforcing emergence. In fact, when an effort is made to influence a complex adaptive system, those seeking to influence become part of that complex adaptive system.

The emergent strategy enables policies to have a broader impact, but, because of their unpredictability, they also restrict the policyowner from establishing high-level outcomes, and to an ongoing re-designing process to deal with emergence.

Emergent strategies are required to:

- bring together multiple other component polices and systems (that may not be under the direct control of the policyowner) to deliver a higher order policy outcome using a systems-of-systems.
- accommodate change in the component policies and systems—policies that display emergent characteristics need shell designs that can accommodate a plug-and-play approach, with component policies being replaced and new policies being added.
- use stewardship, as opposed to direct control.
- use WAVE Planning in lieu of traditional project management planning methodologies.

The emergent strategy is suited to complex policies.

Dealing with Asymmetric Behavior

The detailed design approach of bespoke strategies significantly limits their capability to deal with asymmetric behavior. To be effective, bespoke strategies need to carefully define the policy's language, rules, and regulations so that they cannot be misinterpreted or misapplied.

Evolutionary strategies provide a limited defense against asymmetric behavior through their progressive development, but they are still vulnerable to asymmetric behavior because of their reliance upon fully defining the policy and its delivery processes in advance.

Emergent strategies are designed to deal with change, and respond both proactively (using foresight and systems thinking) and reactively to asymmetric behavior. Policies using emergent strategies are more likely to be complied with, since the use of asymmetric behavior will have limited/short-term effectiveness.

Table 1 shows key characteristics of the three strategies

4. Systems-of-Systems

A systems-of-systems is defined as a set or arrangement of component systems that:

- results when independent and useful component systems are integrated into a larger system that delivers unique capabilities;
- delivers a higher order goal through bringing together multiple component policies and agents;
- are loose-coupled systems where autonomous component policies are brought together to deliver a high order goal, while the autonomous component policies continue to deliver their own specific goals;
- establishes a separate system to enable component policies and agents to work together; and
- does not integrate the component policies or agents.

Distributed ownership of individual components represents a risk problem for any policy systems-of-systems. Since the systems-of-systems policyowner does not control the political process or the component policies, governance becomes significantly more complicated and must change to accommodate the realities of a policy systems-of-systems. Many different organizations have influence over or own pieces of the systems-of-systems, yet it is unlikely that a single organization will own the entire systems-of-systems. Without an overall systems-of-systems governance strategy and process, it is likely that the individual component policyowners will develop policies according to their localized priorities, resulting in negative local effects deriving from the systems-of-systems.

To enable policy systems-of-systems to deliver unique goals, the complex policyowner establishes:

- At the political level, a compelling case to gain and maintain political support. This will often include negotiating trade-offs to obtain the necessary support.
- At the operational level, an umbrella system to enable the component policies to work together. This bringing together of the component policies is done through establishing a shell that allows a 'plug-and-play' approach with the component policies being added, changed, and removed as required, and with these component systems remaining effectively unchanged—the systems-of-systems strategy does not attempt to fully integrate the component policies.

Policy systems-of-systems introduce a new set of issues that have significant implications for governance. The following list of characteristics captures the essence of how a policy systems-of-systems differs from a standalone policy:

To view the electronic version of this journal and this image, scan the code below or visit: http://www.ipsonet.org/publications/open-access/policy-and-complex-systems/ volume-1-number-1-spring-2014

Table 1. Characteristics of Policy Strategies

- Operational independence of the systems: Each system within a systems-of-systems has a "life of its own" and can function effectively and provide useful service without necessarily interacting with other policies.
- Managerial independence of the systems: The individual policies within a systems-of-systems are under different authorities.
- Evolutionary development: The different policies within the systems-of-systems are developed and upgraded on uncoordinated schedules.

Not all systems-of-systems will exhibit all of these characteristics, but it is generally assumed that a systems-of-systems is characterized by these. Although the individual systems within a systems-of-systems are usually considered to have independent operational viability, it is sometimes the case that the systems-of-systems must contain some systems the only purpose of which is to enable the inter-operation of the other component systems. That is, these enabling systems cannot operate outside of the systems-of-systems.

The key aspects for structuring of a systems-of-systems for complex policies are:

- establish an umbrella enabling system that supports the inter-operation of the component legacy policies;
- establish process governance to plan and coordinate inter-operability and emergent change across the systems-of-systems component policies and systems;
- establish a shell structure to enable a 'Plug and Play" approach where component policies can be removed, changed, or added;
- include legacy policies and new policy components;

- change may need to be made in component policies to enable them to effectively operate as a component in a policy systems-of-systems; and
- establish a capability for policy systems-of-systems rapid fielding and emergence. The traditional enterprise capability is based on a sequential model that is not suited to today's emergent world or complex systems-of-systems. Process Governance, WAVE Planning, and Stewardship provide the rapid and agile capabilities required for managing complex policy systems-of-systems.

Types of Policy systems-of-systems

Policy systems-of-systems can take one of the following four forms[9]:

- **Directed**: Directed policy systems-of-systems are those in which the systems-of-systems is created and managed to fulfill specific policy goals, and the constituent policies are subordinated to the policy systems-of-systems. The component policies maintain an ability to operate independently, but their normal operational mode is subordinated to the centrally managed policy systems-of-systems goals.
- **Acknowledged**: Acknowledged policy systems-of-systems have recognized goals, a designated policyowner, and dedicated resources for the policy systems-of-systems; however, the constituent policies retain their independent ownership, objectives, funding, and development and sustainment approaches. Changes in the policy systems-of-systems are based on co-operative agreements between the policy systems-of-systems owner and the component policyowners.
-

- **Collaborative**: In collaborative policy systems-of-systems, the component policies interact more or less voluntarily to fulfill agreed upon central purposes. The central players collectively decide how to provide or deny service, thereby providing some means of enforcing and maintaining standards.

- **Virtual**: Virtual policy systems-of-systems lack a central management authority and a centrally agreed upon purpose for the systems-of-systems. Large-scale behavior emerges—and may be desirable—but this type of systems-of-systems must rely on relatively invisible mechanisms to maintain it.

Meta Systems-of-Systems

According to the OECD, at a fundamental level, the world consists of 11 core systems[10] (refer Figure 14). Each of the 11 core systems has evolved over time to serve a specific need or want of society. Collectively, they form a global meta systems-of-systems (SoS).

- Each of the 11 core systems itself operates as a meta SoS.
- Countries and businesses operate as meta SoS at the national, regional, and local levels.

In government today, there is a need for acknowledged policy systems-of-systems to deal with complex policy issues including multi-jurisdiction policies.

Like directed policy systems-of-systems, acknowledged policy systems-of-systems have recognized authorities and resources at the systems-of-systems level. However, because an acknowledged policy systems-of-systems comprises policies that maintain independent objectives, management, and resources, along with independent development processes, these policy systems-of-systems are largely collaborative in practice. For policies in these systems-of-systems, in particular, their normal operational mode is not subordinated to the policyowner (which is a distinct feature of a directed policy systems-of-systems).

Government policies and funding are still largely ministry-focused, and many policy systems-of-systems do not have authority over the component policies. Typically, they try to address policy systems-of-systems' objectives by leveraging the developments of their component policies, which are normally more long-standing and better supported than the policy systems-of-systems. Consequently, acknowledged policy systems-of-systems, like directed policy systems-of-systems, have objectives, management, and funding without authority over the component policies. Like collaborative policy systems-of-systems, changes in component policies to meet policy systems-of-systems' needs are based on agreement and collaboration, not top-down authority from the policy systems-of-systems owner.

Complex policies are complex meta systems-of-systems that are best understood as having two separate, but integrated systems-of-systems: Complex policy objectives, strategy, and political support; and Complex policy emergent implementation using a systems-of-systems.

---

[9] US Office of the Secretary of Defense, Systems Engineering Guide for Systems-Of-Systems. Version 1.0 August. Director, Systems and Software Engineering Deputy Under Secretary of Defense (Acquisition and Technology) Office of the Under Secretary of Defense (Acquisition, Technology and Logistics), 2008

[10] IBM Global Business Services, The World's 4 Trillion Dollar Challenge. Using a Systems-of-systems Approach to Build a Smarter Planet, 2010.

To view the electronic version of this journal and this image, scan the code below or visit: http://www.ipsonet.org/publications/open-access/policy-and-complex-systems/ volume-1-number-1-spring-2014

Figure 14. World SoS

To view the electronic version of this journal and this image, scan the code below or visit: http://www.ipsonet.org/publications/open-access/policy-and-complex-systems/ volume-1-number-1-spring-2014

Figure 15. Complex Policy Objectives

Complex policy objectives, strategy, and political support

The political systems-of-systems for complex policy addresses (refer Figure 15) the definition of goals, the design, implementation, and ongoing emergent management strategy, and most importantly obtaining and maintaining political support.

Complex policy emergent implementation

The implementation SoS delivers the establishment of the policy's enabling network and machinery of government as well as the ongoing management of the policy and the network (refer Figure 16). This network responds to changes in the policy goals and scope directed from the political systems-of-systems.

Complex policy meta systems-of-systems

The complex policy meta systems-of-systems (refer Figure 17) integrates the political policy systems-of-systems, and the policy implementation and emergent management systems-of systems.

5. Stewardship and Process Governance

Stewardship is generally recognized as the acceptance or assignment of responsibility to shepherd and safeguard the valuables of others.

Complex policies are emergent, use systems-of-systems as their design and implementation structure, and involve multiple independent component policyowners and agents working together to deliver high-level goals. Therefore, governance for systems-of-systems is difficult for the design

and manage mindset of the traditional command and control approach. While the policy systems-of-systems owner establishes high-level goals, the component policyowners and agents cannot be made to adhere to any individual set of goals and rules that are defined. In fact, there may be many component policyowners and agents with a variety of different and, perhaps, competing goals.

Developing stewardship[11] between the policyowner, the component policyowners and agents is a critical aspect for the journey management of complex policies (Refer Figure 18). Stewardship is operationalized through process governance[12] and WAVE Planning. Complex policies are not just 'complex systems' bounded by the fixed rules of interaction between their parts—rather, they are 'complex evolving systems' that can change the rules of their development as they evolve over time.

Process governance provides the stewardship that drives the journey, holds the policy systems-of-systems focused upon the emergent policy goals and supports an emergent strategy (as opposed to maintaining the status quo). Throughout the journey, process governance maintains the strategic focus for the policy as the stakeholders' views change. Process governance proactively uses double loop learning to deal with changes to stakeholder views, and thereby maintains stakeholder alignment, commitment and stewardship. Through process governance, multiple and often opposing views are accommodated, and the policy systems-of-systems owner is provided with genuine control.

When developing a single, standalone policy, the policyowner has directive control and authority within their organizations and can effectively enforce governance over the components they own. Even when multiple organizations are involved, the policyowner must have directive au-

To view the electronic version of this journal and this image, scan the code below or visit:
http://www.ipsonet.org/publications/open-access/policy-and-complex-systems/
volume-1-number-1-spring-2014

Figure 16.Complex Policy Implementation

To view the electronic version of this journal and this image, scan the code below or visit:
http://www.ipsonet.org/publications/open-access/policy-and-complex-systems/
volume-1-number-1-spring-2014

Figure 17. Complex Policy Meta systems-of-systems

To view the electronic version of this journal and this image, scan the code below or visit: http://www.ipsonet.org/publications/open-access/policy-and-complex-systems/ volume-1-number-1-spring-2014

Figure 18. Stewardship

thority through the cabinet or through the department's control over the agencies in a hierarchical manner. Policy ownership of a systems-of-systems is a complex matter, with no single organization being in any position of ownership (and by extension authority) over the whole. Governance is about control, and the issue is how can control be established across systems-of-systems that have distributed ownership? If control is essential to the effective policy systems-of-systems realization, then without sufficient control what will encourage independent organizations to adopt shared goals?

It is difficult to establish control over a complex systems-of-systems precisely because no individual or organization can have total authority—even when it appears that a single authority does exist. For example, a department may create a systems-of-systems with authority for the integration of constituent policies into a systems-of-systems. Theoretically, this new systems-of-systems has some authority over the constituent policies and their associated stakeholders. However, in instances such as this, the owners of the constituent policies and systems inevitably have primary allegiance to their particular stakeholders. Even if owners of constituent policies and systems are unusually committed to the systems-of-systems, a single authority is likely to be ineffective since the size of the overall capability makes it extremely difficult to understand the nuances involved in effective control. Thus, the only alternative is to facilitate collaborative identification and adherence to a shared set of governance processes.

Collaborative systems-of-systems governance involves abandoning the no-

tion of rigid top-down governance of processes, standards, and procedures, and adopting peer-to-peer approaches such as Integrated Process Teams, Partnering, and Connective Planning. Such collaborative systems-of-systems governance is at odds with the natural tendency of government, because it means that the "chain of command" must evolve to a "web of shared interests". Collaborative systems-of-systems governance requires cooperation between separate authorities and agents, even when there is no formal agreement.

The characteristics of collaborative governance for systems-of-systems are:

- **Independent systems-of-systems facilitation**—new responsibilities are needed for policy systems-of-systems owners to act as conveners, and to engage external facilitators to co-ordinate the policy systems-of-systems establishment and ongoing development.
- **Identifying the scope of shared goals**—understanding each party's goals, and agreeing and documenting areas where shared goals can exist and cannot exist. There will be legitimate goal, motivation, and accountability differences. These differences need to be recognized, respected, and understood.
- **Incentives for co-operation**—where there is no directive control, policy systems-of-systems owners need to establish incentive processes to motivate component policyowners and agents to participate cooperatively. Incentive based motivation is most easily achieved with private sector agents where the incentive is linked to Key Performance Indicators.

---

[11] System Stewardship, The UK Institute of Government, 2011.

[12] D. Dombkins, and P. Dombkins, *Contracts for Complex Programs* (Booksurge, Amazon, Group, 2008).

- **Agreeing to shared values**—the parties agree and document the values that they will collaboratively work with. The values and agreed shared goals are documented in a charter against which co-operation is measured.
- **A problem-solving orientation**—a formal process to identify and prioritize both problems and opportunities, and to develop tangible action plans. The problem solving process is repeated periodically.
- **Participation by interested and affected parties in all stages of the decision-making processes**—partnering and the use of integrated policy teams establish democratic processes that facilitate effective problem solving and buy-in.
- **Provisional solutions**—complex policies are recognized as being subject to ongoing revision, which requires willingness to move forward under conditions of uncertainty and to reconsider goals and solutions:
  - Evolution of the component policies: a fundamental characteristic of a systems-of-systems is that its component systems will change at different rates and in an uncoordinatedmanner. At a minimum, governance for evolution should include rules and guidelines for:
    - informing other component policyowners and agents of the changes;
    - coordinating schedules with component policyowners so that those that have to change can do so together (when backward compatibility of interfaces cannot be maintained);
    - developing each policy to insulate it from changes in other component policies; and
  - minimizing the impact to interfaces when changing a component policy.
  - Evolution of the systems-of-systems itself: while evolution of the systems-of-systems may be directed, it will also occur, by default, when new component policies are added. If policies are simply added to the systems-of-systems without forethought, the unanticipated interactions between the various policies will create behaviors that are unanticipated and undesirable. Test and Evaluation methodologies are needed to evaluate systems-of-systems establishment and evolution.
- WAVE Planning provides a methodology to manage complex policy realization.
- **Back to zero**—policies are based upon assumptions and driven by views (subject to bounded rationality). The WAVE Planning methodology uses double loop learning to periodically reassess the policy against changed assumptions and views.
- **Accountability**—traditional top-down oversight may be supplemented or replaced by self-disclosure and shared monitoring.
- **Avoiding problems**—coordination problems can occur at multiple levels within the parties. An escalation ladder is established to expediently resolve issues at the lowest level, and to rapidly escalate problems if they cannot be solved at lower levels.

6. Sensemaking and Foresight

Policies are driven by philosophy, visions, and/or a desire for change. Thus, policies have an intent, one that is shared to different degrees by those participating. This is particularly important in complex policies where agents play a key role in the implementation, delivery, and emergent development of the high-level policy goals. A successful complex policy requires that the agents are able to make sense of the policy individually, in the context of their respective roles, as well as collectively.

Making sense of the situation—sensemaking[13]—begins with putting available information into context and identifying the relevant patterns that exist. Therefore, sensemaking begins with the development of situation awareness.

Situation awareness includes awareness of the policy high-level strategic goals. In the process of developing situation awareness, the policyowner and agents may determine that more information is needed before policy design or policy redesign.

Sensemaking involves more than developing situation awareness—it goes beyond what is happening to include what may happen and what can be done about it.

Sensemaking (refer Figure 19) involves ongoing analysis, modeling, and prediction, across multiple domains (social, information, physical, cognitive, and political).

The need to consider a wide range of effects and the cascades of effects that take place in the multiple domains requires more knowledge, experience, and expertise than when only the policy specific effects are considered.

This is one of the major reasons why effects-based approaches to planning (such as social, economic, political, etc.) benefit from a complex approach to policy.

Foresight

While evidential support is important in policy development, there is a growing awareness that much of the evidential support for traditional strategies and tactics is oftentimes neither valid nor reliable—and this lack of reliable evidential support makes outcomes prediction difficult. This problem with evidentiary support is compounded by the emergent nature of complex policies that are affected by ongoing emergence.

Emergence is in turn complicated by the growing incidence of asymmetric strategies and tactics with corporations and governments seeking to gain strategic advantage by getting around and/or taking advantage of government and international policies.

To succeed in this complex world, governments need a new way of thinking that is in tune with our complex world and where *'uncertainty is the only certainty'*.

No one can predict the future, and herein lies the fundamental weakness in policymaking—in our complex world it is extremely difficult to model real world political, financial, social, economic, technical, and environmental systems. This complexity is made substantially more difficult by the past providing little guidance for predicting the future, asymmetric behavior becoming the norm, and frame-breaking changes occurring regularly.

The best that governments can do in this scenario is to understand that the real world is a complex system, and use this understanding to develop policymaking strategies and methodologies that allow them to develop policies and implementation frameworks that deliver tangible outcomes today, while retaining the capability to in-

---

[13] D. Albrerts, and R. Hayes, Planning: Complex Endeavors (CCRP Publications, 2007)

To view the electronic version of this journal and this image, scan the code below or visit: http://www.ipsonet.org/publications/open-access/policy-and-complex-systems/ volume-1-number-1-spring-2014

Figure 19. Sensemaking

troduce changes without significant rework or interruption to continuity. Not all policies are complex. Therefore, policymakers will be more effective if they purposefully view different types of policies through different lenses (refer to Table 2).

Foresight for complex policies can be developed through modeling, combined with WAVE Planning, connective planning, systems thinking, and agent based modeling. Combined, these methodologies and tools provide an understanding of our complex world, and foresight into complex policy design, implementation, delivery, and emergence. Five toolsets support policyowners in developing foresight: Systems Thinking; Multiple views; Technical Enterprise Readiness Index; Agent Based Modeling; and WAVE Modeling

Systems Thinking

Systems thinking provides policymakers with a range of tools to support design, risk management, strategy selection, and sensemaking. Table 3 allocates appropriate systems thinking tools to each of the policy strategies, and takes into consideration the nature of the policy environment.

Multiple Views

Bounded rationality is one of the greatest risks in policy design. A structured process that looks at policy through multiple views provides the policyowner with a holistic understanding. These multiple views can be developed and integrated using a range of systems thinking tools.

Technical Enterprise Readiness Index

Tools such as the Technology Readiness Level (TRL), Integration Readiness Level (IRL), Systems Readiness Level (SML),

and Enterprise Readiness Level (ERL) provide key inputs into policy development and implementation planning.

Agent Based Modeling

Agent Based Modeling[14] provides complex policymakers with a tool to simulate complex systems-of-systems.

WAVE Modeling

WAVE Planning enables the modeling and simulation of alternative governance, and stewardship strategies for value sustainment in systems-of-systems.[15]

With foresight, governments:

- have voluntarism, and are not easily caught by events outside their control;
- have the ability to steer emergence;
- can proactively feed forward to influence their future; and
- can effectively leverage their legacy systems, while providing a framework that can proactively take up new technologies; and that proactively invest in and take advantage of future technologies.

7. Evidentiary support for Policy Design

Owing to their varying levels of certainty and risk, different approaches to evidence to support decision making are appropriate for the three Policy strategies (Bespoke, Evolutionary, and Emergent).

In an idealized world, decision makers would set clear goals, gather all necessary relevant information related to the problem and desired solutions, and then devise alternatives to meet the goals.

To view the electronic version of this journal and this image, scan the code below or visit:
http://www.ipsonet.org/publications/open-access/policy-and-complex-systems/
volume-1-number-1-spring-2014

Table 2. Different Lenses for Policy Makers

To view the electronic version of this journal and this image, scan the code below or visit:
http://www.ipsonet.org/publications/open-access/policy-and-complex-systems/
volume-1-number-1-spring-2014

Table 3. Systems Thinking Toolset

Alternatives would then be prioritized and choices would be made based on agreed upon criteria. This process would be supported by accurate information, which would reduce the uncertainties and risks in policymaking along with general theories, and would guide the comparison of alternative solutions.

The intent is to improve policymaking through establishing validity between the policy strategy, the level of supporting evidence, and the focus of the policy (high-level or detailed). However, this ideal approach is seldom realized in government.

Policymakers have two distinctly different scientific research methodologies: empirical and grounded—(Refer to Figure 20) available to them:

- Empirical research is based upon theory, predictions (formulas), and experimentation. Theories and experimentation simplify problems through using deductive thinking to focus on a limited number of variables, and ignore the noise from a complex world. Empirical research provides very detailed causal relationships between a small number of variables that can be used to develop very detailed policies (bespoke and evolutionary policy strategies).
- Grounded research focuses on the real world using inductive thinking to develop a holistic system understanding. Complex policies usually have a variety of interacting variables, multiple interdependent processes operating

simultaneously, and exhibit behavioral patterns that are non-linear, recursive, and emergent. The grounded research approach is suited to provide evidence to develop high-level goals and guidance for emergent policy strategies. The WAVE Planning methodology and agent-based modeling provide effective testing and evaluation processes of complex policies.

Evidentiary support for complex policy-owners is provided by both the grounded and empirical methodologies of scientific research, with each of the methodologies providing different computational and modeling processes. Table 4 summarizes the differences between the bespoke, evolutionary, and emergent policy development/implementation strategies.

Policies designs are driven by philosophy, vision, and/or problems. Regardless of the policy driver, policyowners are faced with the issue of policy design. However, depending upon the type of policy (bespoke, evolutionary, or emergent) different approaches to policy design are required.

The heuristics for policy design are:

- Do not plan detail beyond the certainty horizon.
- Bounded rationality will drive policy design.
- Understand the policy holistically before commencing design.
- Understand the policy design cost

[14] P. Acheson, L. Pape, G. Dagli, N. Kilican-Ergin, J. Columbi, and K. Haris, Understanding Systems of Systems Using an Agent-Based Wave Model. Complex Adaptive Systems, Publication 2 Cihan H. Dagli, Editor in Chief. Conference Organized by Missouri University of Science and Technology 2012, Washington DC, 2012.

[15] N. Ricci, A. Ross, D. Rhodes, and M. Fitzgerald, "Considering Alternative Strategies for Value Sustainment in system-of-systems." SEAri Working Paper Series, WP-2012-3-2. Systems Engineering Advancement Research Initiative, Massachusetts Institute of Technology Cambridge, 2013.

To view the electronic version of this journal and this image, scan the code below or visit:
http://www.ipsonet.org/publications/open-access/policy-and-complex-systems/
volume-1-number-1-spring-2014

Figure 20. Different Ways of Thinking

model: designing the policy to a cost, or costing the policy design.

8. Policy Categorization Tool

There are three different strategies for policy design, implementation, and delivery: bespoke, evolutionary, and emergent.

The Policy Categorization Tool (PCAT)[16] provides a tool for governments to categorize policies, and to select: an appropriate strategy for the design, implementation, and delivery of policies; appropriately competent policy leaders and teams; and appropriate governance, rules, feedback, and response for each policy category.

POLICY CATEGORIZATION TOOL

The PCAT Tool categorizes policies into one of five categories (refer to Table 5)

Complex Policies

Increasingly, governments are faced with policies that are not merely complicated, but truly complex. Complex policies involve changes and behaviors that cannot be predicted in detail, although those behaviors and changes can be expected to form recognizable patterns. Complex policies are also characterized by circumstances in which relatively small differences in initial conditions or relatively small perturbations (seemingly tactical actions) are associated with very large changes in the resulting patterns of behavior and/or strategic outcomes.

PCAT1 are policies that are driven by a vision and have the following characteristics:
- high levels of emergence

- high internal system complexity
- high external system complexity
- politically critical

PCAT 2 are policies that are driven by a vision and have the following characteristics:
- high levels of emergence
- high internal system complexity
- high external system complexity
- politically important

Complicated Policies

Complicated policies are characterized by having many parts or actors, and are highly dynamic—that is, the elements of these policies constantly interact with and impact upon one another. However, the cause and effect relationships within a complicated policy are generally well understood, which allows planners to predict the consequences of specific actions with some confidence.

PCAT 3 are policies that are driven by defined outcomes/outputs and have the following characteristics:
- low to medium levels of emergence
- moderate internal system complexity
- moderate external system complexity
- moderate political importance

Traditional Policies

Traditional policies are readily decomposed into definable elements and have cause and effect relationships that are generally well understood, which allows planners to predict the consequences of specific policies with confidence.

PCAT 4 policies have the following characteristics:
- low levels of emergence
- low internal system complexity

To view the electronic version of this journal and this image, scan the code below or visit:
http://www.ipsonet.org/publications/open-access/policy-and-complex-systems/
volume-1-number-1-spring-2014

Table 4. Comparison of Policy Strategies

- low to moderate external system complexity
- moderate political importance

PCAT 5 policies have the following characteristics:
- low levels of emergence
- low internal system complexity
- low external system complexity
- low political importance

The PCAT tool combines contemporary research into complex policy with criteria used within the defense sector for project categorization. The Policy Assessment criteria used by PCAT is detailed in Table 6.

PCAT Scoring and Categorization Summary

Each of the four assessment criteria has multiple sections:

- Internal Policy Complexity:
  - Delivery organization
  - Systems-of-systems complexity
  - Technical complexity
  - Design, implementation, and delivery complexity
- Emergence:
  - Strategic emergence
  - Organizational emergence
- External Policy Complexity:
  - Stakeholder complexity
  - Maturity of policy's external environment
  - Expectations
- Importance:
  - Strategic importance
  - Policy cost

Each of these sub-sections has multiple assessment questions. The PCAT Tool rates each of these questions for importance (from zero for low importance, to 10 for high importance). Individual governments can alter the rating of the questions.

The first step in categorizing a policy is to assess the policy by scoring each question. Each question is scored between low and high (Refer to Figure 21).

The PCAT Tool calculates a score for each of the four criteria, an overall score for the policy, and categorizes the policy into one of five categories (Refer to Figure 22).

9. Integrated Policy Teams

Integrated Policy Teams is a management methodology that integrates all activities from policy concept through to design, delivery, implementation, and emergent development, by using a multifunctional team to simultaneously optimize the policy's realization and to meet cost and performance constraints. (Refer to Figure 23).

The model for Integrated Teams was first developed by the U.S. military for the concurrent development of operational processes and products.[17] In dealing with complex policy systems-of-systems, integrated teams:

- provide a structural design for bringing the multiple component policyowners and agents together to design, realize, and manage the emergent policy systems-of-systems;
- operate at the steering, design, management, implementation, services delivery, compliance, technical, and functional levels;
- are structured to respect the individual

---

[16] D. Dombkins, Complex Project Management (Booksurge, Amazon Group, 2007).

To view the electronic version of this journal and this image, scan the code below or visit: http://www.ipsonet.org/publications/open-access/policy-and-complex-systems/ volume-1-number-1-spring-2014

Table 5. Linking PCAT to Policy Strategy

To view the electronic version of this journal and this image, scan the code below or visit:
http://www.ipsonet.org/publications/open-access/policy-and-complex-systems/
volume-1-number-1-spring-2014

Table 6. PCAT Assessment Criteria

To view the electronic version of this journal and this image, scan the code below or visit:
http://www.ipsonet.org/publications/open-access/policy-and-complex-systems/
volume-1-number-1-spring-2014

Figure 21. PCAT Scoring Process

To view the electronic version of this journal and this image, scan the code below or visit:
http://www.ipsonet.org/publications/open-access/policy-and-complex-systems/
volume-1-number-1-spring-2014

Figure 22. PCAT Assessment Summary

To view the electronic version of this journal and this image, scan the code below or visit: http://www.ipsonet.org/publications/open-access/policy-and-complex-systems/ volume-1-number-1-spring-2014

Figure 23. SoS Integrated Teams

goals of the component policyowners and agents; and

- use partnering and connective planning as supportive processes.

10. Complex Policy—Rules of the Road

- Complex policy objectives are defined in high-level goals that can remain relevant over time.
- Do not define the policy detail beyond the certainty horizon.
- Use multiple systems thinking methodologies to develop a holistic understanding of the policy. These methodologies will provide different views that may be contradictory.
- Emergent behavior occurs in complex policies, where unexpected outcomes occur that cannot be predicted by knowledge of the policy's constituent parts. "Unexpected" means unintentional, not purposely or consciously designed-in, not known in advance, or surprising to the developers and users of the policy.
- The emergent outcomes of a complex policy can result from either the internal relationships among the component part of the complex policy, or as a response to its external environment.
- Complex policies bring together multiple component policies to deliver a higher-order goal.
- Complex policies establish systems the only purpose of which is to enable the inter-operation of the other component policies.
- Complex policyowners need agents outside of their direct control to develop and deliver complex policies. These

agents will adapt policy delivery solutions to their own purposes and local conditions that will themselves change over time.

- Complex program owners operate in an environment where they do not control all of the component policies or agents that impact the policy, and stakeholders have interests beyond the complex policy's objectives.
- Complex policyowners must balance the complex policy's needs and goals with individual component policyowners and agents' needs and goals.
- Policy design, implementation, and delivery must consider and leverage the development plans of the individual systems and establish a governance system to manage change.
- Focus primarily on the end-to-end behavior of the complex policy, and address the constituent systems only from that perspective.
- Use right to left thinking.
- Use a policy design based on open systems and loose coupling to support the addition or removal of component policies, as well as ongoing emergence.

11. References

Acheson, P., L. Pape, N. Kilicay-Ergin, and J. Columbi. 2012. *Understanding Systems of Systems Development Using an Agent Based WAVE Model*. Washington DC: Complex Adaptive Systems, Missouri University of Science and Technology.

Agusdinata, B., and D. DeLaurentis. 2008. "Specification of Systems-of-Systems for Policymaking in the Energy Sector." *The International Assessment Journal* 8 (2):1–24.

---

[17] US Department of Defense, DoD Guide to Integrated Process and Product Development. Version 1.0 February 5, 1996.

Briassoulis, H. 2004. *Policy Integration for Complex Policy Problems: What, Why, How.* Berlin Conference "Greening of Policies: Interlinkages and Policy Integration.

Dagil, C. 2012. *An Advanced Computational Approach to Systems of Systems Analysis and Architecture Using Agent Based Behavioral Model.* Systems Engineering Research Centre.

Desouza, K., and Y. Lin. 2011. "Towards Effective Policy Design: Complex Adaptive Systems and Computational Modeling." *The Public Sector Innovation Journal* 16 (1):article 7.

Dolphin, T., and D. Nash. 2012. *Complex New World: Translating New Economics Thinking into Public Policy.* Institute of Public Policy Research.

Kilicay-Ergin, N., P. Acheson, J. Colombi, and C. Dagl. 2012. *Modeling Systems of Systems Acquisition.*

Lindquist, E. 2011. *Grappling with Complex Policy Challenges.* Australian National University, HC Coombs Policy Forum.

Morris, E., P. Place, and D. Smith. 2006. *System-of-Systems Governance: New Patterns of Thought.* Software Engineering Institute.

Swanson, D., and S. Bhadwal. 2009. *Creating Adaptive Policies.* International Development Research Centre. Sage Publications.

Enhancing ABM into an Inevitable Tool for Policy Analysis

Dr Amineh Ghorbani[A], Dr Francien Dechesne[B], Dr Virginia Dignum[C], Prof. Dr. Catholijn Jonker[D]

Social systems consist of many heterogeneous decision-making entities who create complexity through their interactions. These systems are governed by policies in a multi-scale institutional context. While policy is a top-down instrument, its effect is determined by a bottom-up process, in the sense that the aggregate behavior of the social system is the result of interaction and reasoning on the level of individuals. We argue that understanding social systems at the individual level significantly contributes to understanding and predicting the effectiveness of policies. Given that agent-based modeling (ABM) allows for rich representation of individuals, it is well suited for providing necessary insights for policy analysis. To support this claim, in this paper, we give a systematic overview of the requirements that policy analysis puts forward. By viewing policy analysis as a cycle of activities, we discuss five categories: problem definition, policy evaluation, identification of alternative policies, decision support, and monitoring. Moreover, we evaluate mathematical and computational tools with respect to these requirements. Finally, we propose a list of extensions to ABM for monitoring, decision making, and participatory design in the policy analysis cycle.

Keywords: agent-based modeling, policy analysis, tool selection, policy cycle

1. Introduction

How would taxation on light bulbs or subsidies on LED lamps influence the behavior of consumers toward more energy saving habits? Can investment on manure-based biogas systems improve farming prospects for animal farmers? And, does fining recyclers in a developing country prevent them from hiring children and using dangerous chemicals when they are recycling electronic appliances? These questions all address policy problems, exploring the long-term effect of strategic decisions on the operational behavior of individuals and on the global outcomes of the complex social system.

Policies are rules or instruments guiding actions and decision making by people in order to achieve desired outcomes in social systems. The design of effective policies is a cyclic process of identifying the objective, defining alternative policies, selecting the one that would best address the objective, and finally monitoring and evaluating the implemented policies' effects on the system (Weimer and Vining 2005). Throughout this cycle various tools ranging

[A] Faculty of Technology Policy and Management, Delft University of Technology, The Netherlands

[B] Faculty of Technology Policy and Management, Delft University of Technology, The Netherlands

[C] Faculty of Technology Policy and Management, Delft University of Technology, The Netherlands

[D] Faculty of Electrical Engineering, Mathematics and Computer Science, Delft University of Technology, Delft, The Netherlands

from benchmarking and historical analysis (Scharpf 1997) to computational simulations (Gilbert 2004) are used.

Policies are implemented as top-down decisions but their acceptance is—at least partly—a bottom-up process. This calls for a system understanding at the microlevel in order to find out which of the alternative policies are most effective (Scharpf 1997). Microlevel analysis contributes an insight into the individual's unanticipated adaptive behavior, decision making, and interactions, facilitating the improvement of conditions for effective policy solutions.

The need for micro-level analysis has a good fit with what agent-based modeling (ABM) offers. ABM, as a bottom-up simulation approach, builds artificial societies from individual agents and their interaction, giving insight into how people may react toward different situations (Banks et al. 2000). Compared to other computational approaches such as differential equations and statistical modeling, ABM imposes less assumptions on linearity, homogeneity, normality, and stationarity (Banks et al. 2000). In addition, agent-based models have the power to demonstrate emergent phenomena at system level. This is especially instrumental for policy problems where the influence of individual behavior on system properties is under study (Conte et al. 2001).

However, to use ABM for policy analysis there are additional requirements. For example, for evaluating policy alternatives, the policy analyst also needs means of imposing policies (or rules) to the simulated system in order to study individual reaction and adoption to these impulsions. Therefore, building a system purely from bottom-up may not be entirely instrumental for policy analysis. Furthermore, since the subjects of policy problems are societies with real people, the reliability of an agent simulation and the results it provides are a sensitive issue that require careful evaluation.

The goal of this paper is to show the suitability of ABM as an approach to analyze policy problems and how it can be enhanced to address even more requirements for policy analysis. To achieve this goal, we first explain the policy analysis cycle and introduce the various steps and requirements in the analysis process in Sections 2 and 3. We then introduce the computational tools that are commonly used for policy analysis and reflect on the benefits and drawbacks of each, in Section 4. We explain how ABM can be used as a comprehensive approach for policy analysis and discuss areas for further enhancement in Section 5. Finally, we conclude our findings in Section 6.

2. The Process of Policy Analysis

A policy is a set of principles or rules to guide a social system toward those actions that are most likely to achieve a desired outcome. Policies can be implemented as social norms (e.g., switching off lights when leaving a place which must be internalized by people, for example, through advertisement campaigns), legal impositions (e.g., subsidies and taxes on the different consumer products such as milk, LED light bulbs, etc.) or technological artifacts (e.g., electronic gates at stations).

The practical activities of policy-making and implementation are distinguished from the more reflective activities of policy analysis which aim at determining which alternative policies may most likely achieve desired goals and outcomes. Policy analysis is specifically complex because the consequences of implementing a policy "are the outcomes under external constraints of intentional action" (Scharpf 1997). In other words, human actors are driven by a combination of internal intentions, natural impulses, and/or external factors that make modeling behavior complex.

In the first step the policy analyst verifies, defines, and details the given problem by characterizing the social context in which the problem is embedded and identifying the independent variables that affect policy outcomes. The identification of the problem source and the independent variables is a major milestone in policy analysis because the objective of the problem owner is often either not clear or appears to be in conflict. In fact, most often, different actors view the problem in their own perspective. It is the role of the analysts to understand the positions and influence of various stakeholders and choose the definition that the problem owner/decision maker has control on (Patton and Sawicki 1993). Clarification of the problem takes place with consultation, brainstorming, narratives, and scientific research. Often, the problem is redefined many times during the process of analysis. In the second phase, the policy analyst identifies the criteria that show when the problem is solved or a goal is accomplished. The analyst aims to select those criteria that are central to the problem and most relevant to the decision makers in the implementation process (Patton and Sawicki 1993). This also facilitates the comparison between policy alternatives. During comparison, new criteria may also be identified.

Once the analyst knows the values, objectives, and goals of the stakeholders and the evaluation criteria for judging policies, he can generate alternative policies (Patton and Sawicki 1993) . The list of possible alternatives is usually long since there are many variations and combinations for the policies. Benchmarking and past experience are common approaches for identifying policy alternatives (Scharpf 1997; Patton and Sawicki 1993).

Among policy alternatives, the most appropriate options are selected using the already defined evaluation criteria. The alternatives are compared based on the potential effects and their chain of causation. Since not every policy can be tested with the same method, analysts have access to various methods (e.g., cost–benefit analysis, programming, institutional analysis, and quantitative analysis) to evaluate different policies. It is important to identify economically, technically, and politically feasible alternatives. This is where many institutional analysis theories and frameworks (i.e., IAD (Ostrom 2005), Actor Centred Institutionalism (Scharpf 1997)) are frequently applied. Furthermore, it is important to clarify the distinction between possible policies and to be able to display them to the problem owners. Consultation commonly takes place to increase the efficiency and transparency of policy implementation (Althaus, Bridgman, and Davis 2007).

The final phase of policy analysis is the monitoring, maintenance, and evaluation of the implemented policy. In most instances, the analyst develops implementation guidelines and procedures rather than being involved directly in the implementation of the selected policy. It is important for the analyst to know whether a failed policy could not be implemented as designed or the policy did not produce the desired results because the underlying theory was incorrect (Patton and Sawicki 1993). Therefore, policy analysts are highly involved in the postevaluation of implemented policies. In general, this phase is about monitoring the use of inputs and the achievement of outputs, and evaluating the direct effects and long-term impacts of the policy.

In the next section, we discuss what kind of requirements the different steps of the process put forward for policy analysis tools.

To view the electronic version of this journal and this image, scan the code below or visit:
http://www.ipsonet.org/publications/open-access/policy-and-complex-systems/
volume-1-number-1-spring-2014

Fig. 1. Policy analysis cycle (Patton and Sawicki 1993)

3. Requirements for Policy Analysis Tools

The main objective of policy analysis tools is to support a better understanding of the policy problem and the context in which the problem is situated, and to support the evaluation of policy solutions. To reach this objective, there are several aspects that need to be taken into account. First, even though policy implementation is a top-down procedure, policies affect individuals. It is the combination of individuals' reactions that determines the success of a policy implementation. While for some problems, it may suffice to capture and understand the overall emergent behavior of the population, for others, a deep understanding of individuals, their unanticipated behavior, and decision making and interactions is essential (Scharpf 1997). Therefore, it is important that policy tools provide a suitable level of system analysis to link between individual behavior and global outcomes. Second, to better understand the problem and its context, the policy instruments need to reflect reality to a required extent depending on the type of problem. Therefore, it is important to consider to what extent the underlying assumptions for any tool (e.g., rationality and complete information) match the characteristics of a specific policy problem.

Each step in the policy analysis cycle (Figure 1) has specific requirements which are classified into five areas discussed below:

1. Problem definition
   Policy analysis requires the means to clarify the problem itself including:
   a) Techniques that facilitate communication with domain experts and stakeholders (Moss 2002).
   b) Techniques to parameterize the problem or problematic behavior.
   c) Means of understanding and defining the population. Even though a detailed understanding of individuals may not be a key element for every policy problem, a general understanding of the population that will be affected by the policy is a minimum requirement. In most cases, the context has a large number of active entities and there is very little knowledge about the global interdependencies.
   d) Means of identifying the available resources, processes, physical and environmental characteristics, and boundaries of the system where the policy is conducted.

2. Evaluation Criteria
   Support for policy evaluation includes:
   a) Specific measures such as cost, benefit, effectiveness, and legality. The problem owner provides these measures directly or indirectly.
   b) Means of clarifying, deducing, and confirming measures whether or not provided by the problem owner (Patton and Sawicki 1993) and associating the measure specifications with problem definition.
   c) Tools for identification and consideration of extreme values and worst-case scenarios.

3. Identification of Policy Alternatives
   Identifying alternative policies is closely related to the problem definition and the set of evaluation criteria. To identify policy alternatives, the analyst requires:
   a) Means for identifying the attributes of each policy.
   b) Means of linking policies to evaluation measures.
   c) Inclusion of technical, economical, societal, and political aspects of each alternative (Patton and Sawicki 1993).

d) Tools to display and present alternative policies.

4. Decision Support for Selecting Policy Alternatives

   a) Instruments to distinguish, categorize, and compare policies.

   b) Tools to support participatory decision making.

   a) Means of answering what-if scenarios.

   b) Tools for tracking the behaviors and reactions toward policies, before policy implementation (e.g., gaming and simulation).

   c) Tools for testing extreme values and worst-case scenarios.

5. Monitoring implemented policies

   After implementation, policies can be monitored and evaluated using the evaluation criteria identified in the second step of the cycle. The policy analyst requires:

   a) Tools and methods to compare and illustrate the before-and-after situations in order to evaluate the effects of a policy.

   b) Tools for tracking the behaviors and the reactions.

Besides the specific requirements mentioned above, data collection, data analysis, and research are the common requirements for every step of the process. For an effective policy, consultation is also essential throughout the policy analysis process (Hodge and Davies 2006). There are different levels of consultation; for some projects, public opinion is taken into consideration while for others, this may need to be more limited due to, for example, security reasons (Althaus, Bridgman, and Davis 2007). Furthermore, for selecting any policy instruments, the time constraints that the policy analysts work under need to be considered (Patton and Sawicki 1993).

Policy analysts use various tools in different phases of the policy analysis cycle (e.g., surveys, brainstorming, sensitivity analysis, institutional analysis, etc.) (Patton and Sawicki 1993). It is common practice to select a combination of tools that complement each other for different policy cases. Computational tools are in particular frequently applied to cover more scenarios and possibilities than normally possible with non-computational tools (e.g., scenario writing). In this research, we especially focus on the computational tools that are used for policy analysis. We will compare these tools and reflect on the benefits and limitations of each in order to identify areas for improvement.

4. Computational Approaches for Policy Analysis

Different policy tools focus on different aspects of the policy analysis cycle. Given the importance of computational tools, we introduce the major approaches that are currently in use, namely: Neo-classical Equilibrium Modeling (NEM), Traditional Game Theory (TGT), System Dynamics (SD), Serious Gaming (SG), and Agent-based Modeling (ABM). We then discuss the benefits and drawbacks of each as a policy analysis tool.

Neo-classical Equilibrium Modeling

Neo-classical Equilibrium Modeling (NEM) is a frequently applied tool for market-related policy problems. NEM provides mathematical models of markets and has special focus on maximizing profit, competition, and income distributions in markets through supply and demand (Jones 1965).

Neo-classical models take into account many aspects of a real economy including commodities, production, growth, and money (King, Plosser, and Rebelo 1988). However, they mostly address centralized market economy and therefore are not suitable for other types of decentralized markets.

The underlying assumptions in NE models such as full rationality of parties, complete information, and certainty also create concerns about their reliability on the insights they provide. Although this line of research is gradually moving toward higher uncertainty approaches, rationality of individuals and complete information are the necessary pillars in equilibrium modeling.

Traditional Game Theory (TGT)

Game theory is the most frequently applied tool for understanding actor behavior and decision making in policy problems (Gibbons 1992). The fundamental concepts in game theory are players, strategies, and payoffs. A player may be an individual or a composite actor that is capable of making choices. Strategies are lists of consecutive actions for a player, or functions assigning actions to each decision point of a player on the basis of previous actions by the opponents.

The limited number of actors and outcomes, the joint product of separate choices, and the actors being aware of their interdependence, make game theory useful for policy analysis (Scharpf 1997).

However, there are a number of strong assumptions in TGT that make it less suitable for many policy problems (Scharpf 1997): perfectly rational actors, complete information, self-interest, and unlimited computational and cognitive ability. Another limitation of game theory is that it does not provide a macroperspective explanation of policy choices, which is commonly required for policy analysis (Scharpf 1997). One other limitation of TGT is that the number of interactions between actors is very limited (interactions between three agents (Moss 2001)) while for policy problems, hundreds or thousands of actors may be involved.

System Dynamics

System dynamics (SD) is a computational simulation approach which has its roots in differential equations. With this approach, a system is described using a system of equations with which future states of the system are derived from its current state. In system dynamics (SD), real world problems are represented in terms of stocks, flows, and information. SD ignores single events and entities and takes an aggregate perspective (Borshchev and Filippov 2004).

The ease of use and availability of packages and tools makes system dynamics one of the most popular computer-based analysis tools among policy analysts. However, as the simulations grow bigger, the number of assumptions increases, introducing additional questions of validation to support the reliability of the simulated model.

The high number of assumptions thereby also makes the model less flexible. Essentially, SD is a one-layer approach which means that the focal system is simulated as an indivisible whole. It does not take into account the fact that the actual system consists of individual people and it is their behavior and reaction that actually results in global outcomes.

Serious Gaming

Serious games can be designed to gain insights into policy problems. These types of games are a simulation of real world systems and events where players get the chance to make decisions about virtual events. The purpose of a serious game is to put actors in situations representing reality, in order to understand their decision process and then study the possible outcomes of the aggregation of those decisions. These situations can be virtual (i.e., computer games) or real (i.e., a setting that would represent the real world situation).

Games provide the possibility to learn on multiple levels. While the involved players may learn from the contextual information provided by the game or the decision making as it takes place during the game, useful material is gathered by the designers of the game to solve the underlying policy problem (Raybourn and Waern 2004). Serious games do not necessarily have to be computer-based; they could also be role-plays among human players.

While serious gaming (SG) reflects a great part of real actor decision making, compared to other models, the population that can be considered for a game is normally much smaller than the real population and therefore unreliable to extrapolate to real world scenarios.

Agent-based Modeling

Agent-based modelling (ABM) is a computer-based modeling approach that enables the exploration of the consequences of complex assumptions (Janssen and Ostrom 2006). In ABM, models are inherently bottom-up and decentralized. Therefore, ABM describes those situations where the standard methods of predictive policy analysis are least effective (Moss 2002).

With ABM, it is possible to design irrational agents with incomplete information in relatively uncertain situations.

The main advantage of ABM over other modeling approaches is that it captures emergence, linking individual behavior to system level behaviors. This results in a natural representation of a system's global behavior as well as adding more flexibility to possible outcomes (Bonabeau 2002). However, since ABM is a bottom-up approach to problem solving and the global behaviors of the system are emergent outcomes rather than being implemented into the system (Epstein 2006), techniques for representing policies as top-down structures into the simulation are neither common nor straightforward.

Functionality of the Tools for Policy Analysis

The tools introduced in this section are all used for policy analysis. In fact, in most cases the policy analyst uses a selection of these tools along with the non-computational methods. Therefore, highlighting which part of the policy analysis cycle each tool supports will be informative for choosing an effective combination of the tools. Table 1 shows where in the policy analysis cycle the aforementioned tools can be helpful. The letters in the second column show which requirement of Section 3 is addressed.

NEM can be used to parameterize the policies and make an association between different dimensions using equations. NEM does not support the identification of the resources, processes, characteristics, and boundaries of the system. However, once they are detected, it also helps parameterize these attributes for problem attributes. This also holds for the evaluation measures and policy definition. A limitation of this mathematical method is that it does not facilitate communication with domain experts because mathematical equations are not understandable to everyone. Also, NEM does not help to gain insights into individual behavior and decision making, as it describes the system from a macro perspective. In terms of decision support, NEM can be used to categorize and distinguish policies through mathematical equations. However, since certainty is one of the assumptions in this approach, the answer to what-if scenarios using this approach are not always reliable. This also holds for tracking behaviors because not only the system is analyzed at macrolevel, individuals are considered fully rational with complete information. These assumptions may also not justify answers for certain behaviors and reactions when monitoring the implemented policies.

Unlike NEM, traditional game theory takes an individual-based approach, which provides a means of specifying the population in the problem definition. However, TGT is about outcomes rather than individual behavior. Therefore, it is not the most suitable tool for tracking individual behaviors and reactions for selecting a policy or monitoring an implemented one. While TGT can be used to define evaluation measures and identify extreme values and worst case scenarios through computing equilibria, as a standalone tool, it has other limitations. For example, it does not provide a test bed for participatory decision making unless it is used with serious gaming (SG). TGT does not support the identification of policy alternatives either: there is no way of identifying the attributes for policy alternatives and it is infeasible to link policies to evaluation measures.

System dynamics (SD) is a computer simulation approach that makes use of differential equations. Therefore, all the benefits of mathematical descriptions, such as formulating policies and their attributes and defining evaluation measures, are facilitated with SD. Owing to the availability of tools, displaying and presenting various policies is practical. In addition, SD like other simulation approaches enables tracking of system behavior. However, the major limitation of SD is that the system is not viewed as a collection of individuals. Therefore, it is infeasible to gain insights into populations and the decision-making behavior of individuals and thus not possible to track behaviors and reactions at individual level toward a policy. Nonetheless, the general processes and outcomes are traceable. Furthermore, instead of identifying boundaries and resources for a policy problem, to make a system dynamics simulation, these aspects need to be defined beforehand.

Serious gaming (SG) is one of the most useful tools to define a policy problem. It also facilitates the definition of evaluation measures and identification of their link with the problem definition. When the players become involved in a serious game, they are able to place themselves in the situation to find out how policies would affect them. This facilitates the identification of the association between policy alternatives and evaluation measures. The limitations of serious gaming (SG) are all related to the limited number of players in a game which is normally much smaller than the number of agents in the system in which the policy would actually be implemented. This limitation makes it difficult to:

– rely on the results for what if scenarios,
– test extreme values and worst case scenarios, and
– track reactions toward policies before and after a policy implementation.

Agent-based modelling (ABM) is similar to SG, with the difference that the people in serious games are represented as artificial agents in ABM. ABM covers many of the benefits of SG because both tools deal with populations of individuals. Since ABM is aimed at existing systems (Moss 2002), and is descriptive rather than predictive (Lempert 2002), it is instrumental for comparing and illustrating the before-and-after situations of a policy implementation. In addition, ABM also provides valuable insights into the emergent outcomes of policy implementation which are the result of individual behaviors and reactions. In fact, ABM combines the benefits of the aforementioned tools. However, there are still areas for improvement.

The issues related to emergence in simulations are (1) the type of emergence: are they physical (e.g., traffic patterns)? or social (e.g., punishment for stealing)?, and (2) the detection, analysis, and possibly control of emergence. In current ABM research, physical emergence is extensively addressed in simulations especially when using visual tools such as Netlogo. It is, however, more difficult to address social emergence because it is not always visually recognizable in a simulation.

One other drawback of ABM is that since the systems are simulated from bottom-up, there is no straightforward method to simulate the social or technical environment of the system, or to define the boundaries. This also makes it difficult to include the technical, economical, societal, and political aspects of policies into simulations. Currently, these factors are either not considered in the simulations or they are modeled as part of the agents. Modeling social structures within agents is not realistic because agents and structures are interrelated but separate concepts. The primary consequence of simulating the combination of the two as one entity is that we would not be able to study the influence of social structures on individual behavior and the system as a whole. Furthermore, social structures are also influenced by individuals. If they are modeled within agents, it is not possible to model global changes in these structures and observe how they evolve and diminish, and how new structures emerge. In current agent-based models, it is difficult to explicitly display and present policies because of the inability to model social structures. Therefore, being able to model policies as a purposive design of social structure also facilitates their presentations.

final drawback of ABM for policy analysis is related to participatory model development. Although simulation results can be communicated to problem owners to facilitate participatory decision making, building collaborative agent-based models is not a common process.

5. Enhancing ABM for policy analysis

Although ABM addresses various requirements for policy analysis, there are still areas for further extending its applicability in this area. In this section, we discuss how ABM can be improved at each of the requirement levels of Section 3.

Enhancements for Problem Definition in Policy Analysis

While there are visual tools and techniques for ABM that facilitate communication with domain experts by showing results of simulation runs, consultation with stakeholders for problem clarification is not a built-in facility for ABM. There-

To view the electronic version of this journal and this image, scan the code below or visit: http://www.ipsonet.org/publications/open-access/policy-and-complex-systems/ volume-1-number-1-spring-2014

Table 1. Policy analysis approaches and the type of problems they can be used for

NEM: Neo-classical Equilibrium Modeling, TGT: Traditional Game Theory, SD: System Dynamics, SG: Serious Gaming, ABM: Agent-based Modeling

fore, ABM for policy analysis requires tools for involving stakeholders when developing the agent-based model. This can be achieved by combining serious games and real actors into agent-based models (Castella, Trung, and Boissau 2005; Guyot and Honiden 2006).

The integration of ABM and SG would also facilitate and improve the parameterization of the problem or problematic behavior. While it is possible to develop highly sophisticated intelligent agents who are capable of making realistic decisions for their actions and interactions, the agents are still predictable to a great extent. Incorporating real actors in the agent-based model covers uncertain and unanticipated behaviors.

Enhancements for Dealing with Evaluation Criteria in Policy Analysis

Evaluation of policies is important because a faulty choice can have expensive consequences in terms of health, money, time, and security. Agent-based modelling (ABM) can have several added values in terms of policy evaluation. First, involving real actors in simulated scenarios in an agent-based model can help them identify measures. Second, by providing consistency between policy measures and those evaluations performed on the agent-based models, the results of the simulated system can be highly reliable for the policy analysts. Currently, verification and validation of agent-based models is more geared toward the actual software model rather than real world implications. Finally, using serious games and involving problem owners and domain experts in agent-based simulations would also facilitate the definitions of evaluation measures.

Enhancements for Dealing with Policy Alternatives

Many ABM tools and packages provide visualization facilities (e.g., Tisue 2004; North, Collier, and Vos 2006). However, it is highly instrumental if ABM tools have explicit policy representation so that it is possible to enable/disable each policy alternative in order to observe the effects. As we previously discussed, having an explicit structure for policies re- quires the incorporation of top-down social structures in agent-based models rather than building them purely from bottom-up (Conte et al. 2001).

Another issue for studying policy alternatives is the exploration of the emergent consequences of a policy implementation. As previously discussed, emergent behavior in a social system (i.e., the global reaction toward an implemented policy) is different compared to other emergent properties existing in physical and natural systems which are commonly recognized as emergence in ABM (Epstein 2006). Emergence in a social system is recognized and identified by the individuals and reacted on, while in other types of emergence, the individuals (e.g., birds in a flock) are not conscious about the emergent structure they have created. For example, in a flock, the birds form a shape while they are not aware of the flock shape and do not make an effort to influence the shape in any particular way. They do, however, try to position themselves according to their neighbors. In a social system on the other hand, an individual recognizes an economic crisis (an emergent pattern). He tries to change the situation if powerful enough or adjust his own status according to the global situation rather than his own surroundings and neighbors.

For policy analysis, not only artificial agents should be able to recognize a policy change in the system, they need to identify the global behaviors and adjust their behavior accordingly (i.e., adaptability). For example, if inefficient light bulbs are banned in one country, an agent may start buying LED lamps because they are the only ones available in the market. Another consequence of such a policy may be the formation of black markets. The rich cognitive agent must be able to recognize this emergent phenomenon and make decision on whether to continue buying LEDs or buy banned light bulbs from the emergent black market.

The emergence and evolution of social structures is studied both in the social sciences (Axelrod 1986; Janssen 2005; Smajgl, Izquierdo, and Huigen. 2010) and computer science (Holland 2001; Smajgl, Izquierdo, and Huigen 2008). This line of research can be further enhanced to explore the effect of imposing policies on the emergence of social structures.

Enhancements for Decision Support for Policy Selection

ABM is a bottom-up approach which models individuals rather than top-down principles (Epstein 2006). Policy analysis by definition is about imposing guiding principles into a social system. Therefore, ABM for policy analysis should be a combination of bottom-up and top-down model development to facilitate explicit and elaborate policy comparison and evaluation. Using System Dynamics (SD) techniques is one way of facilitating this combination (Scholl 2001; Castella et al. 2007). Furthermore, participatory decision making is a new line of research in ABM where enhancements can be highly instrumental for selecting policies (Barreteau, Bousquet, and Attonaty, 2001).

Finally, advances in verification and validation of agent-based models are required to be able to trust the results of comparison between policy alternatives using ABM. Results from agent-based simulations are difficult to interpret due to their size and complexity. Even more, as there is usually no test using empirical data, most evaluations do not normally go beyond a proof of concept (Janssen and Ostrom 2006).

Enhancements for Monitoring Implemented Policies

Improving cognitivity in agents can provide more insights into why people give certain reactions toward an implemented policy. Furthermore, the artificial intelligence literature which provides means of implementing cognitive agents needs to be more accessible to social scientists. Currently, this line of research provides sophisticated tools that are difficult to comprehend and use by social scientists and policy analysts who are less familiar with computational sciences.

6. Conclusion

The goal of this research was to explore the potential of ABM as a tool for policy analysis. To perform this research, we presented a systematic overview of the policy analysis cycle to identify the requirements it puts forward. We then compared various tools that are used for policy analysis, including ABM, to identify the benefits and drawbacks of each.

The comparison between the different tools provides our hypothesis that ABM can indeed be considered as an inevitable tool for policy analysis under the condition that some enhancements are made. Therefore, by using the results of our comparison, we identified areas where ABM can be enhanced:

– Enabling participatory model development to enhance problem definition and identification of evaluation criteria.
– Enabling the detection, exploration, and control of social emergence to empower the selection of policy alternatives by gaining more insights into possible outcomes.
– Combining bottom-up and top-down modeling, so that agents can make decisions and act in a more realistic environment where social and physical structures are present and influence their behavior. This would support the selection process of policy alternatives by also providing explicit representation of policies as social structures.
– Enabling conceptual as well as computational evaluation of agent-based model to increase the reliability of such models.
– Increasing the accessibility of agent-related research for social scientists and policy analysts who are less experienced in computational sciences.

In conclusion, we believe that because of the importance of individual-based study of policy problems and to make use of the computation power of simulations, ABM is one of the most instrumental tools for policy analysis. To enhance ABM in the identified areas, combining this approach with SG and SD can be effective. In addition, uncertainty analysis, case loading, and data calibration are some of the methods that need to be focused on when choosing alternative policies using ABM (Bankes 2002). Also, complex agent-based models result in enormous amount of data which require powerful data analysis tools.

Bibliography

Althaus, C., P. Bridgman, and G. Davis. 2007 *The Australian Policy Handbook*. Sydney: Allen & Unwin.

Axelrod, R. 1986. "An Evolutionary Approach to Norms." *The American Political Science Review* 1095-1111.

Bankes, S.C. 2002. "Agent-based Modeling: A Revolution?" *Proceedings of the National Academy of Sciences of the United States of America* 99 (Suppl 3): 7199.

Banks, J., S.C. John, L.N. Barry, and M.N. David. 2000. *Discrete-Event System Simulation*, Third Edition. Upper Saddle River, NJ: Prentice-Hall, Inc.

Barreteau, O., F. Bousquet, and J.M. Attonaty. 2001. "Role-playing Games for Opening the Black Box of Multi-agent Systems: Method and Lessons of Its Application to Senegal River Valley Irrigated Systems." *Journal of artificial societies and social simulation* 4 (2): 5.

Bonabeau, E. 2002. "Agent-based Modeling: Methods and Techniques for Simulating Human Systems." *Proceedings of the National Academy of Sciences of the United States of America* 99 (Suppl 3): 7280.

Borshchev, A., and A. Filippov. 2004. From System Dynamics and Discrete Event to Practical Agent Based Modeling: Reasons, Techniques, Tools. In *The 22nd International Conference of the System Dynamics Society*. Citeseer.

Castella, J.C., T.N. Trung, and S. Boissau. 2005 "Participatory Simulation of Land-use Changes in The Northern Mountains of Vietnam: The Combined Use of An Agent-based Model, A Role-playing Game, and A Geographic Information System." *Ecology and Society* 10 (1): 27.

Castella, J.C., S. Pheng Kam, D. Dinh Quang, P.H. Verburg, and C. Thai Hoanh. 2007. "Combining Top-down and Bottom-up Modelling Approaches of Land Use/Cover Change to Support Public Policies: Applica- tion to Sustainable Management of Natural Resources in Northern Vietnam." *Land Use Policy* 24 (3): 531-545.

Conte, R., B. Edmonds, S. Moss, and R.K. Sawyer. 2001. "Sociology and Social Theory in Agent Based Social Simulation: A Sym- posium." *Computational & Mathematical Organization Theory* 7 (3): 183-205.

Epstein, J.M. 2006. *Generative Social Sci- ence: Studies in Agent-based Computational Modeling*. Princeton University Press.

Ghorbani, A. 2013. *Structuring Socio-tech- nical Complexity—Modelling Agent Systems Using Institutional Analysis*. PhD thesis, Delft University of Technology.

Gibbons, R. 1992. *Game Theory for Applied Economists*. Princeton University Press.

Gilbert, N. 2004. "Agent-based Social Sim- ulation: Dealing With Complexity." *The Complex Systems Network of Excellence* 9 (25): 1-14.

Grimm, V., U. Berger, F. Bastiansen, S. Eli- assen, V. Ginot, J. Giske, J. Goss-Custard, T. Grand, S.K. Heinz, G. Huse, et al. 2006. "A Standard Protocol for De- scribing Individ- ual-based and Agent-based Models." *Eco- logical Modelling* 198 (1–2): 115-126.

Guyot, P., and S. Honiden. 2006. "Agent- based Participatory Simulations: Merging Multi- agent Systems and Role-playing Games." *Journal of Artificial Societies and Social Simulation* 9 (4).

Hodge, W., and G. Davies. 2006. Evaluating Policy With a Modified Policy Cycle–The NSW Healthy School Canteen Strategy. In *Australian Evaluation Society International Conference*, 4–7.

Holland, J.H. 2001. "Exploring the Evolu- tion of Complexity in Signaling Networks." *Complexity* 7 (2): 34-45.

Janssen, M.A. 2005. "Evolution of Institu- tional Rules: An Immune System Perspec- tive: Parallels of Lymphocytes and Institu- tional Rules." *Complexity* 11 (1): 16-23.

Janssen, M.A., and E. Ostrom. 2006. "Em- pirically Based, Agent-based Models." *Ecol- ogy and Society* 11 (2): 37.

Jones, R.W. 1965. "The Structure of Simple General Equilibrium Models." *The Journal of Political Economy* 73 (6): 557-572.

King, R.G., C.I. Plosser, and S.T. Rebelo. 1988. "Production, Growth and Business Cycles: I. The Basic Neoclassical Model." *Journal of monetary Economics* 21 (2–3): 195-232.

Lempert, R. 2002. "Agent-based Modeling as Organizational and Public Policy Simu- lators." *Proceedings of the National Academy of Sciences of the United States of America* 99 (Suppl 3): 7195.

Moss, S. 2001. "Game Theory: Limitations and An Alternative." *Journal of Artificial So- cieties and Social simulation* 4 (2): 2.

Moss, S. 2002. "Policy Analysis From First Principles." *Proceedings of the National Academy of Sciences of the United States of America* 99 (Suppl 3): 7267.

North, M.J., N.T. Collier, and J.R. Vos. 2006. "Experiences Creating Three Implementations of The Repast Agent Modeling Toolkit." *ACM Transactions on Modeling and Computer Simulation* (TOMACS) 16 (1): 1-25.

Ostrom, E. 2005. *Understanding Institutional Diversity,*. Princeton University.

Patton, C.V., and D.S. Sawicki. 1993. *Basic Methods of Policy Analysis and Planning,* Vol. 7. Prentice Hall Englewood Cliffs, NJ.

Raybourn, E.M., and A. Waern. 2004. Social Learning Through Gaming. In *CHI'04 Extended Abstracts on Human Factors in Computing Systems*, ACM, 1733-1734.

Scharpf, F.W. 1997. *Games Real Actors Play: Actor-centered Institutionalism in Policy Research*. Westview Press.

Scholl, H.J. 2001. Agent-based and System Dynamics Modeling: A Call for Cross Study and Joint Research. In *System Sciences, 2001. Proceedings of the 34th Annual Hawaii International Conference*. IEEE.

Smajgl, A., L. Izquierdo, and M.G.A. Huigen. 2010. "Rules, Knowledge and Complexity: How Agents Shape Their Institutional Environment." *Journal of Modelling and Simulation of Systems* 1 (2): 98-107.

Smajgl, A., L.R. Izquierdo, and M. Huigen. 2008. "Modeling Endogenous Rule Changes in an Institutional Context: The Adico Sequence." *Advances in Complex Systems* 11 (2): 199-216.

Tisue, S. 2004. Netlogo: Design and Implementation of a Multi-agent Modeling Environment. In *Proceedings of Agent* 2004. Citeseer.

Weimer, D.L. and A.R. Vining. 2005. *Policy Analysis: Concepts and Practice.*

Policymaking in an Information Wired Environment: Realigning Government and Governance Relationships by Complexity Thinking

Claudio Inguaggiato[A], Sylvie Occelli[B]

One core issue in policy making is the management over time of the relationships between the inside and outside government functioning. Although many societal changes are modifying these relationships, they also offer new possibilities. The kind of systemic learning enabled by an increasingly information-rich environment provided by new sociotechnical systems is one of it. In this context, the case of the Piedmont region is discussed where, because of the fragmentation among the government bodies, devising effective government/governance relationships for service delivery is becoming an increasingly severe policy problem. An effort is made to show how an application of a social network analysis can help in addressing the problem, i.e. by prompting a shared reasoning among different government bodies and investigating the range of aggregation opportunities for local municipalities.

Keywords: sociotechnical systems, systemic learning, government–governance relationships, social network analysis.

1. Introduction

To govern means to share authority, ideas, and information with partners as well as with rivals. The system of relationships underlying it encompasses not only public organizations and institutions (government), but also methods and instruments for governing (governance) (OECD 2011).

Although the complexity features of government and governance are by no means a novelty in political and organizational studies (see for example, Conklin 2006; Rittel and Webber 1973; van Dijk and Winters-van Beek 2009), technological and societal changes in the last decade, as well as the current turmoil in the economy, call for further advances in the approaches of analysis (Dennard, Richardson and Morçöl, eds. 2008; OECD 2009; Peach 2004; Wallis 2011).

[A] Coordination Unit in Regione Piemonte, Corso Regina Margherita, 174, 10152, Turin, Italy.

[B] IRES-Istituto di Ricerche Economico Sociali del Piemonte, Via Nizza 18, 10125, Turin, Italy.

[1] Indeed, as explained by NESTA (2008), innovation has never been a main concern in the public sector as:
a. the extent of mandated changes, such as those imposed by legislation or political changes; indeed, this is considered as the main factor for change to occur in the public sector. This is clearly reflected in the ICT uptakes in the Piedmont municipalities, where improvement took place with boots and straps according to legislation (see PICTO 2012);
b. the weakness of ecological forces of competition and the risk aversion attitude, compared with the private sector, which would produce higher survival rates of existing public organizations;
c. the pursue of (maximization of) public value which makes outputs of government programs often diffi-

The recent interest about innovation in public sector reflects[1] an attempt to cast new light on the government/governance issues (see, for example, Navarra and Cornford 2007; Gil-Garcia 2012; Maier-Rabler and Huber 2011; OASIS 2011; Talbot 2008). Basic arguments put forward in the debate argue that innovation would result from an increased variety in the delivered services. Variety, in fact, is produced by the inclusion of a greater number of diverse and proactive actors as well as by a wider set of ICT-enabled services. The availability of new widespread and accessible service outcomes, then, could help in meeting people's increasingly differentiated needs, thus improving the rate of success in achieving government effectiveness and efficiency (Atkinson and McKay 2007).

This is but a reflection of a growing awareness about the need to develop a whole government approach (OASIS 2011; OECD 2011) in which the inclusion of the many relationships between the public sector and their users is a core requirement to cope with the complexity of policymaking, and devise more effective policy actions.

Although acknowledging the opportunity to have a system-wide approach to the government/governance relationships can be regarded as a major contribution in complexity thinking, its implementation in policy practices is still at a design stage (Rhodes et al. 2011).

Coping with the different points of view and motivations by the main actors involved in policymaking, and namely by government organizations, societal partners and scientists, is one main problem to be tackled. Government, who is becoming progressively aware (i) that it has no monopoly on public authority, (ii) that its resources are shrinking, and (iii) that its actions can be more effective in concert with others, is mainly concerned with how to better leverage policy actions (OECD 2011).

Partners (the citizens, the firms, and the non-government organizations (NGOs)) who, as a result of the increasing relevance of ICT networks and social networking tools, are gaining increasing confidence in their relational capabilities (Fedorowicz and Sawer 2012; Murray, Caulier-Grice, and Mulgan 2010; Sawyer 2005), look for government openness and inclusion in the decision-making process (Maier-Rabler and Huber 2011).

Scientists, concerned with the development of ICT empowered policy modeling tools, are challenged to bridge expert and folk domains, and create a more innovative prone human community (Occelli and Semboloni 2011).

Actually, devising a whole government approach requires one to handle these interacting viewpoints and help in establishing more effective government and governance relationships.

This paper aims at giving evidence to the opportunity of developing such an approach, by emphasizing primarily the point of view of government actors, and namely of a group of agents, whose actions are informed by and inscribed in public institutions[2].

---

cult to assess, thus preventing to have clear indications of the created benefits.
The last issue, in particular, has recently stimulated a number of enquiries to define what innovation is about and how to measure it, according to the different types of services and tiers of government organizations (national versus local) (see Australian Government Department of Innovation, Industry, Science and Research 2011; NESTA 2008; Bloch, et al. 2009).

[2] Recalling the public institution role means that the controlling function of government—which include the means by which government policy is enforced and the mechanism for determining the policy itself — has also to comply with the commitment to its social purpose, i.e. seeing to the management of collective goods, promoting the value of public good.

Arguments build upon the past five years experience gained in participating in the activities undertaken by the Piedmont ICT Observatory (PICTO) for accompanying the deployment of the broadband regional program.

The results of these activities show that ICT pervasiveness is progressively creating new types of sociotechnical (system) infrastructures[3] which affect both government efficiency and service delivery and have an impact on the whole policy production process as well. The PICTO studies also reveal that for those system infrastructures to deliver their potential, changes are needed in the ways government actors (at the different institutional levels) engage into their functioning, and manage the government/governance relationships.

To provide ground to the arguments, in the next section, the problem of overcoming the fragmentation among Piedmont municipalities in order to improve service delivery is mentioned. To sharpen the discussion, some results of the applications of social network analysis are discussed which allow us to get deeper insights into the problems. Then, in Section 3, the implications of these applications are briefly reviewed, as they illustrate how adopting a complexity thinking perspective could help in realigning the government/governance relationships

In the final section some summarizing remarks are put forward and an effort is made to highlight the main priorities for this realignment.

2. Reinforcing ICT regional capability: a network approach to the aggregation of municipalities in Piedmont

2.1 Background

Over the past five years the Piedmont Regional Administration has supported an inclusive ICT development, addressing digital gaps in disadvantaged locations. Several initiatives were carried out by a 100 million € program (see www.wi-pie.org), meant to deliver broadband to rural areas, widespread and interoperable e-Government services, while stimulating participative e-Governance.

Progress in the program implementation has been regularly monitored by PICTO since 2006, through yearly surveys on broadband coverage and ICT take up by firms, households, and local authorities (municipalities) (see www.osservatorioict.piemonte.it). Comparative analyses of regional ICT penetration were also carried out, based on the available national and European statistics about information society.

PICTO studies showed that the broadband program gave a fundamental impulse to the establishment of a sociotechnical infrastructure widely diffused in the sub-regional areas. After the program completion in 2010, Piedmont was among the most advanced Italian regions for the delivery of digital services[4].

---

[3] Whereas the notion of Socio Technical Systems (STS) has a longstanding tradition in organizational studies, the boost of ICT is stimulating a revival of interest in its application (see Occelli 2012). This is also acknowledged in recent European policy documents, where ICT progress is considered as a main factor for the transformation of the so-called soft infrastructure, i.e. a mix of institutions and services producing those intangible assets which make the social and human capital so important in fueling the socioeconomic resources of an area (SCF Associated Ltd 2009).

[4] In spite of the distance which still separates Piedmont from the more advanced northern European regions, advancements are but positive, in particular when regarded against the overall regional profile and the current uncertainties of the economy (PICTO 2012).

The impact of the broadband program on the whole regional fabric was noticeable but varied considerably across the various organizations.

Large size enterprises, which traditionally are technology frontrunners, were the first to benefit from broadband services. Notwithstanding they account for the larger share of the regional production basis. Medium and small size firms had more difficulties in exploiting these services, because of organizational impediments, sector specializations, and/or sociocultural constraints.

Citizens' familiarity with broadband and Internet usages increased sharply only when broadband roll up was completed, e-Government services became widespread, and new ICT tools, such as wireless and mobile applications, were fully marketable.

Although the development of e-Government services was a main goal of the regional broadband program, it occurred with boosts and straps, according to the evolution of the national agenda and Italian public administration laws[5].

As for the latter, what PICTO reports contributed to make it explicit was that, in most cases, ICT government initiatives had been too narrowly defined as a means to enhance the efficiency of transactions. Studies also pointed out that a large majority of government organizations, and notably local authorities (municipalities), were unable to exploit, or at least to properly handle, the cascade of changes produced by ICT applications.

To help sharpen the questions two applications of social network analysis were carried out, on the assumption that a system oriented approach meant to investigate the patterns in the relationships among ICT services and among the organizations entitled to their delivery can provide further insights.

Attention is focused on municipalities as these local authorities have a main responsibility in managing ICT services. Furthermore, in Piedmont, there are 1206 municipalities, consisting of a few larger cities (the province head cities) and a majority of small and very small municipalities (80% has less than 5000 inhabitants). Improving the coordination between local authorities, therefore, turns out to be worthwhile for delivering appropriate service levels to the resident population.

2.2 A social network analysis of ICT (based) services by Piedmont municipalities

As mentioned above two applications of social network analysis were carried out.

The first (CASE A) aims to investigate the patterns in the relationships among ICT services. In order to make progress in service delivery, in fact, attention should be paid at better tuning the ICT-supported changes introduced in the back office operations with those carried out in the front office as these are likely to be more sensi-

---

[5] To date, almost all municipalities and government offices in the region are equipped with the basic ICT infrastructures and services (broadband, certified email, digital signature, and institutional websites). The interactivity level of online services however is still under developed and limited to the provision of fill-in forms to prompt administrative procedures. The most widespread online service is population registry self-certification, followed by property tax payment, which is also the most widely available one among the transactional services. ICT is highest in core administrative back office services, such as taxes, demographics, and financial services. These services are often managed inside the administration. For a large number of municipalities ICT equipments are perceived as expensive as they need investments which can be afforded only by the larger administrations.

tive to the new service requirements raised by citizens.

The second (CASE B) explores the possibility to enhance the capabilities of service delivery, by creating larger communities as a result of the aggregation of smallest municipalities.

CASE A: Investigating patterns in ICT services

The analysis is based on the local authority survey carried out by PICTO in 2011 among a sample of 189 municipalities. In addition to gathering data about ICT equipment and applications, the survey enquired about ICT presence in the back office activities and investigated some aspects of the changes necessary to improve service delivery (see, PICTO-CRC 2012).

The social network analysis focused on the relationships among the following types of characteristics/initiatives existing in the municipalities:

a) initiatives for improving back office operations, such as those dealing with norms revision, civil servants' competence, interoperability, etc.;
b) action domains initiatives for improving front office activities, such as those concerning users' needs, quality of service, and the promotion of service functionality;
c) quality of broadband access.

As the capability of local authorities in providing services to their residents depends to a large extent on the municipality size, this turns out to be a main constraining factor to the change possibilities. In the analysis, a distinction has therefore been made between large (with more than 5000 inhabitants) and small (with less than 5000 inhabitants) municipalities.

The graphical representation in Figures 1 and 2 provides an account of these relationships, for large and small municipalities, respectively...

They show that certain cohesion exists among the front office action domains and among the (back office) improvement initiatives. On the contrary, relationships between the front and back office improvement initiatives appear relatively weaker. This suggests that municipalities have a limited understanding about how to link improvements in the front office activities with those in the back office operations.

Larger municipalities, those with more than 5000 inhabitants (Figure 1) consider improvements in all the front office activities as primary actions to be carried out. Compared with the small municipalities, furthermore, their perception about the possibility to connect the front office action domains and back office improvements is higher. Improvements in the quality of service, in particular, are clearly perceived as being influenced by upgrades in service access and better competences of civil servants.

For small municipalities, broadband access is still a main issue. As shown in Figure 2, in fact, the quality of broadband connection (ADSL) plays a major role for improving the quality of services and for better targeting users' needs.

CASE B: Service integration

The difficulties in linking improvements in the front office activities with those in the back office operations to deliver better service are likely to become particularly excruciating at the local level, as a consequence of the shrinking financial resources and limited capability of most small size municipalities. A strategy to be pursued is to create larger communities by

To view the electronic version of this journal and this image, scan the code below or visit: http://www.ipsonet.org/publications/open-access/policy-and-complex-systems/ volume-1-number-1-spring-2014

Figure 1. Large municipalities: relationships between quality of broadband access (gray symbol), (front office) action domains (red symbols) and back office improvement initiatives (blue symbols) for population service delivery (2011) (*)

(*) The graph has been obtained from the UCINET software for network analysis and refers to a sample of 189 municipalities (152 small, 37 large). Relationships have been normalized by number of municipalities. The tie color shows the number of municipalities which share the attributes associated with the nodes.

ADSL: quality of broadband connection; NEEDS: users' needs; QoS: quality of service; PROMO: promotion of service functionality; NORMS: revision of norms/laws; ACCESS: improving the access to service; SIMPLE: reducing administrative burdens for service usage; INTEROP: improving the interoperability of service among the national, regional, and local authorities; EMPLOYEE: improving civil servants' competence.

To view the electronic version of this journal and this image, scan the code below or visit:
http://www.ipsonet.org/publications/open-access/policy-and-complex-systems/
volume-1-number-1-spring-2014

Figure 2. Small municipalities: relationships between quality of broadband access (gray symbol), (front office) action domains (red symbols), and back office improvement initiatives (blue symbols) for population service delivery (2011)
(see note in Figure 1)

putting together the smallest municipalities[6].

Although a regional law, providing the general criteria for the aggregation has been recently enacted, the process by which this assemblage will take place is still undefined. On the one hand, in fact, any genuine spatial grouping proposed by the regional authority, may be viewed as a top down initiative, aimed to rationalize public spending but likely to be irrespective of the local situations. On the other hand, it is also evident that alternative bottom-up initiatives by which municipalities would aggregate themselves on an opportunistic basis will require lengthy and thorny negotiations (not guaranteeing spatial consistency at the regional level).

In this situation, the regional government is confronted with a twofold problem:

1) it has to leverage its authority in such a way as to avoid the negative consequences associated with either deliberated top down or spontaneous bottom up initiatives,
2) and it has to assume its responsibility in making the aggregation process as smooth and effective as possible.

Some encouraging, although weak signals exist which open up new possibilities for addressing the problem.

First, PICTO findings suggest that some of these possibilities will stem from the progressive consolidation of the sociotechnical infrastructure implemented by the regional broadband program. As the notion of sociotechnical infrastructure is gaining momentum, the opportunity it offers for information delivery across the regional system is also growing.

It is expected, in fact, that the information potentials[7] yielded by its functioning (and namely by the widespread usage of the various governmental web portals and user applications encroaching on it), will enable a setting in which a shared (system) learning by the various actors involved in the aggregation process can take place (see, Mitleton-Kelly 2011).

Second, it is also felt that in order to activate this learning, a reflexive loop among municipalities and regional government is necessary (see Aaltonen 2007); besides providing information to the different actors, it would account for their different goal seeking behaviors, and facilitate the discussion of the emerging clustering proposals.

To prompt the establishment of this reflexive loop, a preliminary investigation of a set of municipality aggregations (of the 1206 municipalities) has been made. Established for administrative purposes or for managing service delivery and community planning, the investigated aggregations are:

- Provinces, which divide the regional territory into eight local areas;
- Territorial Pacts, aggregating half of the municipalities in 16 larger communities consisting of approximately 32 municipalities;
- Areas for Integrated Projects aggregat-

---

[6] Indeed, the need to overcome municipality fragmentation is a long-standing problem in Italy and since the 1990s several efforts have been undertaken by researchers and governmental bodies to address it.

[7] It is worth underlining here that in Piedmont concern about information provision and access has institutional roots in a principle of the Piedmont Regional Constitution which states that: information (about the programs and acts of the regional government) is a prerequisite to democratic participation; the Region will ensure its widest diffusion and the broadest pluralism of the media backend and user rights.

ing about 60% of the 1206 municipalities in 18 areas containing about 42 municipalities;

• Integrated territorial programs, resulting from the aggregation of 80% of the municipalities in 29 areas, consisting of the average of 32 municipalities.

On using the UCINET software for social network analysis, Figure 3 shows the intensity of participation of the municipalities to the different spatial clusters, distinguishing also the province they belong to.

The network representation makes it possible to identify some spatial clusters which—depending on the constraints imposed by the morphology of the geographical area—reflect legacy features, inherited from the collaborations municipalities have had in the past for socioeconomic, functional, or planning reasons.

Let us show some details by examining Figure 3 more closely. The spatial aggregation at the top (the light blue circle cluster) represents the municipalities in the VCO province, a mountainous border area in the north-eastern part of Piedmont; it reflects the existence of very tight connections among local authorities that are used to working together but have no ties with other local areas (municipalities) in Piedmont (being close to the Lombardy region, in fact, they have stronger relationships with the local authorities of this region).

The spatial aggregations encircled in red (including orange and violet nodes) identify the Piedmont Wine Area consisting of a set of municipalities in the Cuneo and Asti provinces that run the wine business and have very close relationships.

3. Complexity thinking and government–governance relationships

The two SNA applications, mentioned above, are but examples that give evidence about the types of system relationships underlying a problem, enrich the perspectives of analysis, and can support more effective efforts for problem solving.

As for the ICT service delivery, the advantages were mainly analytics. The SNA application helped to elicit the fact that difficulties exist in aligning front office and back office activities necessary for delivering more effective ICT-based population services. It also made it apparent that these difficulties are greater for small municipalities, thus pointing out that technology changes cannot neglect the context in which they take place.

The SNA application to the thorny problem of municipality aggregation was more exploratory. It allowed us to experiment with a possibility to frame the issue by means of a different (innovative) perspective and prompt the development of complementary analytical approaches, in the GIS and MAS domains.

In both cases, the applications are also examples of how, building upon complexity thinking, the utilization of a cognitive mediator artifact (in this case the SNA applications) (see Occelli 2010) would encroach upon a policy practice, thus increasing the intelligibility of the problem at hand (Morin and Le Moigne 1999).

While in scientific debate the argument may appear trivial, in the policy practices it is almost unknown. Civil servants and decision makers in (Piedmont) government organizations are barely beginning to be aware of it, spurred lately by the uncertainties of an economy in turmoil.

To view the electronic version of this journal and this image, scan the code below or visit: http://www.ipsonet.org/publications/open-access/policy-and-complex-systems/volume-1-number-1-spring-2014

Figure 3 Intensity of participation to the clusters of Piedmont municipalities (*) (*) The shape of the nodes represents the numbers of aggregations a municipality belongs to (up triangle=1, square=2, and circle=3). The color shows the province in which the municipality is located (red=Turin, orange=Cuneo, dark green=Alessandria, light blue=V-CO, light green=Biella, yellow=Novara, dark blue=Vercelli, and violet=Asti). There are 76 municipalities who do not belong to any clusters and are not shown in the representation.

What is clearly perceived, on the contrary, is the heavy burden caused by the increasing complicatedness of everyday policy activities. In this situation, as shown by PICTO analyses (PICTO 2012), the pursuit for innovation and management of ICT pervasiveness are often considered as bureaucratic accomplishments which make the government–governance relationships even more cumbersome.

However, the opportunity of a novel perspective to bear the government burdens and leverage the ICT potential is peeping out[8]. For it to gain momentum in government organizations while taking advantage of the tenets of complexity thinking[9], some issues deserve further attention and are briefly mentioned in the following. Although by no means exhaustive, we hope that they can pave the way for other contributions and help in stimulating additional insights.

A) Extending the perspective of observation of a policy problem.

There is a need to look at problems in a different way in order to counter the overwhelming complicatedness of many policy practices. How this should be done is a longstanding issue and several suggestions have already been made. According to Maeda's laws of simplicity, for example, the crucial aspect in sharpening a problem is to leverage one's design capability by "subtracting the obvious, and adding the meaningful" (Maeda 2006). Other scientists contend that an enhanced approach would result from a process of coevolution in the knowledge perspectives of the involved people (see Mitleton-Kelly 2011). Insights from PICTO studies suggest that such an extension would, ultimately, ensue from the widespread usage of social-based web applications which themselves convey a novel way to appreciate phenomena; not only do they provide manifold information about a certain problem, but they also show how other observers, with different points of view and analytical capabilities, regard and reason about that problem. Interpreted, situated, and exchanged information therefore are additional information chunks which may turn out to be even more valuable than the original one (see Eversole 2011).

As government actors are more and more confronted with the need to couple their own (internal) view of a problem, with the many other (external) views, the role of cognitive mediation artifacts (models) is going to be increasingly important. The point to note in this respect, however, is not so much what kind of methods/ models is going to be the most successful in linking the internal and external views. Rather, as already emphasized in Occelli and Semboloni (2011), the point is what

---

[8] The opportunity to revise conventional advisory system for coping with governance change is also emphasized in Craft and Howlett (2012).

[9] To properly expose the tenets of complexity thinking goes beyond the scope of this paper. For the sake of the present discussion, it may suffice to say that they emerge from the needs of line of enquire in which the consistency requirements commanded by a system approach is specified enough to put them in practice and accommodate the needs of those who have to take actions (Rhodes et al. 2011). The approach is therefore trans-disciplinary and requires (Montuori 2008): (a) a focus that is inquiry-driven rather than based on disciplines, thus calling for a knowledge that is pertinent to the object of inquiry in relation to the purposes of action; (b) an emphasis on the construction of knowledge, thus paying attention at the underlying assumptions through which disciplines construct knowledge; (c) an understanding of the organization of knowledge in situated contexts; and (d) the integration of the knower in the process of inquiry.

knowledge project, underlying the application of a certain artifact within a certain context, is expected to deliver the most in establishing, reinforcing, and enriching that linking.

In the Piedmont case study concerned with service integration, for example, the knowledge project component underlying the social network application had two main aims: (a) to provide a shared reasoning tool among different government offices to investigate the issues of municipality aggregation, and (b) to establish a setting where a constructive dialogue around the various facets of the aggregation issue can take place. A regional government initiative, engaging the different actors to treat the municipality aggregation problem by a system approach, promotes the development of a common "object of discourse", which may be conducive to a more participatory and responsible clustering process.

B) Empowering the government actors

Although the extension of the observation perspective is a general requirement for making the government–governance relationships easier, how this extension is appropriated and used by government actors is an additional question. Being embedded in a more fluid context where there is an increasing variety of partners (citizens, NGOs, and scientists), they need to develop a capability to properly extract and mold the available information, in order to undertake their accomplishments[10].

An aspect often overlooked is how for government actors this capability eventually develops. This has two main facets.

The first, and one hot topic of discussion for the last two decades, relates to data availability: easy, secure, reliable, inexpensive, accessible, and timely data, in fact, are key data features in supporting this capability. By yielding a large amount of new type of data, the extension of the policy perspective mentioned above is likely to contribute substantially to it. However, in front of the unprecedented ICT-related data growth, there is a risk that, without convenient cognitive mediator artifacts, government actors be stacked in a paradoxical situation in which notwithstanding this growth their knowledge capability does not expand but may even be curtailed.

A second aspect is related to how, in practical usage, government actors get hold of data and are able to give significance to them (transform data/information into knowledge) for the task they have to undertake[11]. This is largely unexplored, and too little attention has been paid in the past to the role of (the semantic component of) cognitive mediation artifacts in supporting this appropriation process in policy practices.

Indeed, this acknowledgement explains why in most (Italian) government offices the awareness of those cognitive mediator tools is low and their diffusion is

---

[10] These are manifold and may span across different aspects such as: (a) the type of policy activities they refer to (whether procedural or substantial) and their time horizon (whether they are short- or long-term initiatives); (b) the level/type of accountability associated with a certain accomplishment, whether financial, administrative, or informational (see the recent debate on open data); (c) the type of stakeholders/beneficiaries involved.

[11] We assume that a continuum exists in information usage, insofar, depending on the user/task, we can distinguish between raw data, information (organized data), and knowledge (appropriated information by a user for carrying out a certain task). We also make the hypothesis that the user is willing to update his/her knowledge potential.

limited[12]. In this respect, a claim is made that future technological and methodological developments would not solve the problem unless they are able to properly deal with how the delivered information is tailored to and accompanies the specific tasks government actors engage in.

4. Concluding Remarks

Acentral topic of this paper is that ICT supported knowledge flows among the different actors can become a foundational (new) infrastructure for policy activity and service delivery (see Whitworth 2009; Whitworth and Whitworth 2010). This information wired sociotechnical system encroaches upon the many relationships a system can establish as a result of its representation capability, decision-making processes, and organizational patterns (Gil-Garcia 2012; Occelli 2012). From the policy point of view, it empowers changes in the government and governance relationships as it allows government actors to timely reconfigure their actions, meet user needs, and deliver higher performance system functionality.

The fact that any human organizations will increasingly rely on ICT gives support to the arguments made in OECD (2011) that ICT usage should extend from disseminating information to establishing relationships between inside and outside government, thus making the linking between government and governance more effective in improving the viability of communities and society.

In this respect, the role and functions of complexity-based cognitive mediation artifacts are going to be more and more

important as they become an integrant part of the sociotechnical system. Although limited, to a small part of the system, the preliminary investigation carried out in Piedmont shows that the effort to develop such an approach is possible and worth being undertaken.

Of course, as the usage of these artifacts affects the whole socioinformational linkages the overall pattern of the government–governance relationships will also be continuously reshaped. Maintaining openness and flexibility while guaranteeing robustness of the government–governance relationships over time, therefore, will raise challenging research and policy issues.

PICTO research and the Piedmont case study suggest that, from the point of view of government, some issues are likely to deserve priority attention:

a. efforts of extending the policy perspectives, by complexity thinking, should be primarily aimed at favoring inter-organizational linkages, among the different government offices, at the different institutional levels. As ICTs are transversal to all government departments and policy domains, they can no longer be considered as plugged in factors to be dealt with in isolation. The fact that their usage forms hybrid complex sociotechnical policy bundles requiring cooperation by the different government departments should be reiterated and the arguments for handling them by means of a trans-disciplinary approach popularized (Fuerth and Faber 2012);

b. the significance of information in policy practices is a main topic to address for empowering government actors. In

---

[12] Of course, there are other reasons for that: the relatively low permeability to ICT diffusion; the lack of scientific competences of civil servants; the general cultural inertia which so far has hampered the possibilities to undertake innovative action procedures in the public sector (see Occelli 2007).

particular, the functions cognitive mediation artifacts can play in appropriating existing data and in supporting routinely versus not routinely tasks (such as those motivated by unforeseen citizen needs or emergency situations) need to be further investigated;

c. finally, the experience gained by government actors in carrying out ICT-supported (complexity based) own policy activities should be shared. Exploiting knowledge flows stemming from interpreted information, such as good practices and stories about implemented policy initiatives (see for example Boero and Occelli 2009), can accelerate the empowering process and help in avoiding pitfalls.

References

Aaltonen, M., 2007. "The Return to Multi-Causality." *Journal of Futures Studies* 12 (1): 81-86.

Atkinson, R.D., and A.S. McKay. 2007. *Digital Prosperity*. Washington: ITIF. http://www.innovationpolicy.org.

Australian Government Department of Innovation, Industry, Science and Research. 2011. "Measuring Innovation in the Public Sector: A Literary Review." http://www.gos.gov.uk/497296/docs/191913/237644/rss8.pdf (accessed December 2011).

Bloch, C., L. Lassen Jorgenses, M.T. Norm, and T. Bundgaard Vad. 2009. "Public Sector Innovation Index. A Diagnostic Tool for Measuring Innovative Performance and Capability in Public Sector Organisations, Damvad." http://www.damvad.dk (accessed November 2011).

Boero, R., and S. Occelli. 2009. "Knowledge, Models and Policy Actions: The Potentials of Case Based Reasoning." In *Planning, Complexity and ICT*, eds. G. Rabino, and M. Caglioni. Firenze: Alinea, 185-194. http://www.assystcomplexity.eu/db/pdf/books/Libro_ICT.pdf.

Boon, F., L. Gerrits, and P. Marks. 2012. "Public Administration in Complexity." In *COMPACT I: Public Administration in Complexity*, eds. L. Gerrits, and P. Marks. Litchfield Park: Emergent Publications, 1-12. http://emergentpublications.com/%28S%28ayvtkzp0fgzkbaf4ippap-pyl%29%29/documents/9781938158018_contents.pdf (accessed January 2013).

Conklin J. 2006. Wicked Problems and Social Complexity. In: *Dialogue Mapping: Building Shared Understanding of Wicked Problems*, ed. J. Conklin. Chichester: John Wiley & Sons, 3-40 (see also http://cognex-us.org).

Craft J., and M. Howlett. 2012. "Policy Formulation, Governance Shifts and Policy Influence: Location and Content in Policy Advisory system." *Journal of Public Policy* 32: 79-98.

Dennard, L.F., K.A. Richardson, and G. Morçöl, eds. 2008. *Complexity and Policy Analysis: Tools and Concepts for Designing Robust Policies in a Complex World*. Goodyear, AZ: ISCE Publishing.

Eversole R. 2011. "Community Agency and Community Engagement: Re-theorising Participation in Governance." *Journal of Public Policy* 31: 51-72.

Fedorowicz J., and S. Sawer. 2012. *Desiging Collaborative Networks. Lessons Learned from Public Safety*. ISBM Center for the Business of Government. http://www.businessofgovernment.org/report/designing-collaborative-networks-lessons-learned-public-safety.

Fuerth, L.S., and E.M.H. Faber. 2012. "Anticipatory governance. Practical upgrades." http://www.gwu.edu/~igis/assets/docs/working papers/Anticipatory Governance Practical Upgrades.pdf.

Gil-Garcia, J.R. 2012. *Enacting Electronic Government Success: An Integrative Study of Government-wide Websites, Organizational Capabilities, and Institutions.* New York: Springer.

Maeda J. 2006. *The Laws of Simplicity, Massachusetts Institute of Technology.* Cambridge, MA: IT. http://stephaniagomez.files.wordpress.com/2011/12the-laws-of-simplicity1.pdf

Maier-Rabler U., Huber S. 2011. ""open": The Changing Relation Between Citizens, Public Administration, An Political Authority." *jeDEM* 3 (2): 182-191. http//www.jede.org.

Mitleton-Kelly, E. 2011. "Identifying the Multi-dimensional Problem Space & Co-creating an Enabling Environment." *Emergence: Complexity & Organization* 13 (1-2): 3-25.

Montuori A. 2008. Foreword: Edgar Morin's Path of Complexity. In: *On Complexity.* ed. E. Morin. Cresskill, NJ, USA: Hampton Press, vii-xiiv.

Morin E., and J.-L. Le Moigne. 1999. *L'intelligence de la complexité.* Paris: L'Harmattan.

Murray R., J. Caulier-Grice, and G. Mulgan. 2010. *The Open Book of Social Innovation.*

NESTA. http://www.nesta.org.uk/library/documents/Social Innovator 020310.pdf (accessed January, 2012).

Navarra D.D., and T. Cornford. 2007. *The State, Democracy and the Limits of New Public Management: Exploring Alternative Models of E-government.* London: London School of Economics and Political Science, WP 155.

NESTA. 2008. *Innovation in Government Organizations, Public Sector Agencies and Public Service NGOs.* LSE Public Policy Group.

OASIS 2011. *Transformational Government Framework Primer Version 1.0.* OASIS. http://www.erisa.be/about/Brochures/TG.pdf (accessed October, 2011).

Occelli, S. 2007. "Assessing an Urban Model application to the Piedmont to the Piedmont Region: cui prodest?" Paper Presented at the STOREP Meeting, 3-4 Giugno, Pollenzo.

Occelli, S. 2010. Reconciling Tempus and Hora: Policy Knowledge in an Information Wired Environment. Paper Presented at IC3K 2010, *Second International Joint Conference on Knowledge Discovery.* Valencia, Knowledge Engineering and Knowledge Management, October 23–28. http://www.scitepress.org/DigitalLibrary.

Occelli S. 2012. "Socio Technical Systems and Policy Activity: Some Evidence From the Piedmont Region", *International Journal of E-Planning Research* 4: 59-72. http://www.igi-global.com/journal/international-journal-planning-research-ijepr/44994.

Occelli S., and F. Semboloni. 2011. "Bridging Expert and Lay Knowledge in Policy Making Activities: Which Role(s) for Models?" Paper presented at *the Satellite Meeting on Policy Modelling*. Vienna, ECCS 201, September 14–15.

OECD. 2009. Applications of Complexity Science for Public Policy: New Tools for Finding Unanticipated Consequences and Unrealized Opportunities. http://www.oecd.org/science/scienceandtechnology-policy/43891980.pdf

OECD. 2011. *Government at a Glance 2011*, OECD Publishing. http//dx.doi.org/10.1.1787/gov_glance-2011-en.

Peach, I. 2004. *Managing Complexity: The Lessons of Horizontal Policy-Making in the Provinces Saskatchewan Institute of Public Policy*. Regina, Saskatchewan: University of Regina. http//:www.uregina.ca (accessed May 2011).

PICTO. 2012. Le ICT nella costruzione della Società del Piemonte. Rapporto 2011, Ires, Torino. http//:www.osservatorioict.regione.piemonte.it.

PICTO-CRC. 2012. I Comuni nella Società dell'Informazione. Rapporto 2011. http//:www.osservatorioict.piemonte.it/it/images/phocadownload/prodottiosservatorio/i%20comuni%20nella%20societ%20dellinformazione%202011.pdf.

Rhodes M.L., J. Murphy, J. Muir, and J. A. Murray. 2011. *Public Management and Complexity Theory*, New York: Routledge.

Rittel H. W. J., and M. M. Webber. 1973. "Dilemmas in a General Theory of Planning." *Policy Sciences* 4 (2): 155-169.

Sawyer, K.R. 2005. *Social Emergence: Societies as Complex Systems*. Cambridge, USA: Cambridge University Press.

SCF Associated Ltd. 2009. A Green Knowledge Society. An ICT Policy Agenda to 2015 for Europe's Future Knowledge Society, Bucks, UK. http//:http://camfordassociates.com/wp-content/uploads/2010/11/A-GREEN-KNOWLEDGE-SOCIETY_CREATIVE-COMMONS_WEB.pdf

Talbot C. 2008. *Measuring Public Value. A Competing Values Approach*. London: The Work Foundation. http://www.theworkfoundation.com (accessed January 2012).

van Dijk J., and A. Winters-van Beek. 2009. The Perspective of Network Government. The Struggle Between Hierarchies, Markets and Networks as Modes of Governance in Contemporary Government. In ICTs, *Citizens & Governance: after the Hype!*, eds. A. Meier, K. Boersma, and P. Wagenaar. Amsterdam. IOS Press Series, Amsterdam, 235-255.

Wallis, S. E. 2011. *Avoiding Policy Failure: A Workable Approach*. Litchfield Park: Emergent Publications.

Whitworth B. 2009. "The Social Requirements of Technical Systems." In *Handbook of Research on Socio-Technical Design and Social Networking Systems*, eds. B. Whitworth, and A. De Moor. PA, USA: Hershey, 3-22.

Whitworth B., and A. P, Whitworth. 2010. "The Social Environment Model: Small Heroes and the Evolution of Human Society". First Monday, 15, 11. http://firstmonday.org/htbin/cgiwrap/bin/ojs/index.php/fm/article/viewArticle/3173/2647.

Wi-Pie, http://www.wi-pie.org.

Dissolution of a Global Alliance: War or Peace

Vinogradova Galina[A] & Serge Galam[B]

This work investigates the effect of the dissolution of a global alliance in a collective of individual countries where the alliance, together with its antagonist counterpart, has previously generated stable coalitions. The model rests on the global alliance model of coalition forming inspired from Statistical Physics. Instabilities are a consequence of primary bond based interactions among rational actors and the stabilization is due to new interactions produced by the opposing global alliances. The stability consequences of the dissolution of one of them keeping the other one active are formally investigated within the confines of the model. Two landmark historical cases—the collapse of the Soviet Union and recent Syrian internal conflict—are reviewed. The results shed a new light on the understanding of the complex phenomenon of fragmentation, which may follow the dissolution of a stabilizing alliance.

Keywords: Social models, Statistical Physics, Coalition Forming, Coalition Stabilization, Political Instability.

1 Introduction

This work investigates the effect of the dissolution of a global alliance in the case where two opposing alliances were coexisting producing a stable configuration in a collective of individual countries. The focus is on the effect of fragmentation and instability among the countries in the coalition that have been previously sustained by the dissolved alliance. While the presentation addresses the coalition forming and its eventual fragmentation in an aggregate of countries, the discussion and the results can be applied to any type of political, social, or economic collectives.

We rely on the model developed by Vinogradova and Galam (2013) to describe coalition forming driven by global alliances among countries as rational actors. Countries are coupled with short range in-

teractions that form coalitions under the influence of external fields produced by the global alliances. The conditions for the stabilization of the coalition forming under both unique and multiple factors of influences on their interactions have been singled out.

Coalitions are formed from the attraction or repulsion forces acting between the countries. The latter are determined by the superposition of both the countries' spontaneous interactions, motivated by the static primary bilateral propensities of historical origins and the globally induced exchanges based on a planned profit. Each country chooses the coalition aimed to increase its individual benefit from the interactions with the linked neighbors. Contradictory associations into coalitions due to independent evolution of the primary historical propensities result in instability of the coalitions. The endeavor of the coun-

[A] CREA—Center of Research in Applied Epistemology, Ecole Polytechnique, Palaiseau, France

[B] CEVIPOF—Center for Political Research, Sciences Po and CNRS, Paris, France

tor separated by "/" are given in the square brackets. The example thus illustrates a series of transitions suggesting an infinite cycling as follows.

The figure illustrates a possible branch of configuration transitions (from the left to the right) suggesting an infinite cycling, as follows. In the first configuration, where actor 1 has the maximal gain (+5), the unsatisfied actor 3 makes a change expecting for its maximal gain in a later step. As a result, 1 loses its maximum down at (+1) and 2 gains its own (+4). Prospecting to get back its maximal gain, actor 5 makes a change. This new configuration is the one that yields the expected maximum (+3) for actor 3. At this configuration, actor 2 makes a change to gain an immediate improvement bringing the system back to the initial state with its symmetrical reversal equivalent (the reverse state-colors in the figure). It is interesting to observe that in the case of limited one-step rationality actors, the above system is stable in the third configuration: no actor can observe an immediate improvement of its gain.

Theoretically, the instability of the system of rational actors is defined as the situation when in any configuration of the actors' states there is an actor which is able to forecast an improvement of its gain. The well-defined geometrical terms of the instabilities read as follows. Denote a circle of actors by C and the actors composing the circle by 1, 2, …,k.

If there is a closed circle of actors on which the product of total propensities is negative,

$$\prod_{i,j \in \Omega} p_{ij} < 0 \qquad (2)$$

then the system is unstable.

The negative product on a circle implies an unpaired negative coupling where two neighbors are found to be connected both through positive and negative branches in the circle. This fact creates an everlasting competition between the neighbors for the exclusive arrangement to ally with the positive branch. The actors thereby continuously shift their respective choices producing the instability.

2.2 Global Alliance Model of the Coalition Forming

The global alliance model starts from a global concept, which represents an external field polarizing the interests of the countries. This leads to the emergence of two opposing global alliances. The countries attach themselves to one or to the other based on their pragmatic interests with respect to the global principle. The new interactions, while favoring either cooperation or conflict, stimulate contributions to the countries' mutual propensities. The new prospects unify or separate the countries based on the pragmatic motivations, which in combination with the historical concerns allow other distributions of coalitions.

We denote the two global opposing alliances by M and C, where M unifies the countries that support the global concept and C unifies its opponents. Actor I's individual disposition to the alliances, which is determined by the countries' cultural and historical experiences, is represented by the rational actor's parameter of natural belonging εi, where $\varepsilon i = +1$ if the actor has natural attraction toward alliance M and $\varepsilon i = -1$ for C.

By making a choice among the two possible state values $S_i = +1$ and $S_i = -1$, actor i chooses to belong to either alliance M or C. Countries i and j's choices of one or the other alliance creates new exchanges that define additional propensity between the countries. The propensity is determined by the amplitude G_{ij} of the exchanges in the

To view the electronic version of this journal and this image, scan the code below or visit:
http://www.ipsonet.org/publications/open-access/policy-and-complex-systems/
volume-1-number-1-spring-2014

Figure 2: A branch of transitions in an unstable system of three conflicting rational actors. The actual gain and the maximal gains of each actor separated by "/" are given in the square brackets. The example illustrates a series of transitions suggesting an infinite cycling as follows. The unsatisfied actor 3 makes the change expecting for its maximal gain in a later step which makes 1 to lose its maximum and 2 gains its own. Prospecting to get back its maximal gain, actor 1 makes a change which yields to 3 the expected maximum. Then, actor 2 makes a change to gain an immediate improvement which brings the system back to the initial state, though in its reverse symmetrical setting.

direction $\varepsilon_i\varepsilon_j$ and favors either cooperation or conflict.

The overall propensities between the countries, including both the historical inclinations and the new globally induced propensities, are determined as follows:

$$p_{ij}=J_{ij}+\varepsilon_i\varepsilon_j\,G_{ij} \qquad (3)$$

Respectively, the net gain of actor i is

$$H_i=S_i\Sigma_{j\neq i}\,(J_{ij}+\varepsilon_i\varepsilon_j\,G_{ij})S_j \qquad (4)$$

In the presence of external incentives of the global alliances, the countries' associations into coalitions are adjusting with regard to the new propensities, bringing in a planned feature into the coupling with respect to the spontaneous interactions based on the primary historical propensities.

2.3 Stabilization by Factors of Interest

When referring to the system of countries, a precise factor of countries' interest produces particular dispositions to the present global alliances. Those dispositions determine the countries belonging to the alliances and encourage the new exchanges aligned with that factor. The appropriate amplitudes of the exchanges produce a uni-factor stabilization of coalitions among the countries.

Given two opposite global alliances M and C and the active factor of countries interests G that produce the countries' belonging parameters $\{\varepsilon\}_1^N$, the globally induced propensities are $p_{ij}^{total}=J_{ij}+\varepsilon_i\varepsilon_j\,G_{ij}$.

In real cases, several factors of countries' interests can be active to the global concept—along with religious concerns; the concept may impact economical, ecological, moral, political, and other interests. Accordingly, distinct interests simultaneously influence the interactions between the countries in different ways by inducing specific interactions. The appropriate amplitudes of the exchanges produce the multi-factor stabilization of coalitions among the countries.

Given two active factors of countries' interests G and K producing the respective belonging parameters $\{\varepsilon i\}_1^N$ and $\{\beta i\}_1^N$ globally induced propensities are generated as follows:

$$\begin{aligned} p_{ij}^{total}&=J_{ij}+\varepsilon_i\varepsilon_j\,G_{ij}+\beta_i\beta_j\,K_{ij}\\ &=J_{ij}+p_{ij}^{G}+p_{ij}^{K} \end{aligned} \qquad (6)$$

where

$$\varepsilon_i\varepsilon_j G_{ij}\equiv p_{ij}^{G}$$
$$\text{and } \beta_i\beta_j K_{ij}\equiv p_{ij}^{K}$$

The general multi-factor case can be represented, with no restriction on the generality, through the two-factor form: one of the factors unifies the amplitudes of all the positive new coupling and the other unifies those of all the negative ones. According to Equation (2), the stability terms read as follows:

A system is stable if and only if for any circle Ω in the system,

$$\Pi_{i,j\in\Omega}\,p_{ij}^{total}\geq 0 \qquad (7)$$

Stability space is defined to be a set of all the globally induced interactions $\{(G_{ij},K_{ij})\}_{i,j}$ such that the effective propensities $p_{ij}^{G,K}$ satisfy the above stability condition.

3 Dissolution of a Global Alliance

Produced by the polarization of countries' interests through their natural belongings, the global alliances lead to emergence of new propensities between the countries, which generate stability for particular amplitudes. Once the stability is achieved, the system remains stable for some time—in reality, political, economic, or other interests and motivations are not static, they are subject to evolutionary changes.

When those propensities change, completely or partially, they may exhaust the incentive effect of a global alliance putting the respective countries, for which the stability prevailed during the existence of the alliance, back to their primary geographic-ethnic bonds. Depending on the distribution of the attraction to the global alliance and the amplitudes of the globally induced interactions, the associated coalition exhibits different effective resistance to the dissolution—the robustness of the stability that prevailed during the existence of the alliance.

Formally, the weakening of a global alliance is the weakening of the respective natural belonging parameters of countries by some multiplier $\alpha \in [0, 1]$. The total dissolution takes place when $\alpha = 0$, which sets the natural belonging parameters to zero.

The weakening of global alliance, being generally a dynamic process, should be expressed in terms of dynamic weakening parameter $\alpha(t)$, which is a continuous or discontinuous function of time. The weakening introduces a dynamical aspect into the initially unchanged model in which changes of the primary propensities are negligible.

Definition 1 (Weakening of a Global Alliance). *Given two actors i, j and global alliance M that descends, assume without loss of generality that actor i naturally belongs to the global alliance M. Then, the weakening of the alliance is expressed through the following change of the actors' mutual propensity:*

$$p_{ij}^{total}(t) = J_{ij} + \varepsilon_i \varepsilon_j \, G_{ij} \, \alpha^i(t) \quad (8)$$

The robustness of the stability is naturally determined by the proximity of the new interaction amplitudes to the boundaries of the stability space. We can conclude from Formula (8) that while stability depends on the sign of the total propensity, its robustness depends on the value of the additional, externally induced propensity G_{ij}.

It can be observed from Formula (8) that, taken for all the pair of countries, leaving the closed area of the stability space is always abrupt. This fact explains that in reality, dissolution tends to be followed by unexpected and brutal bursts of conflict.

In this work, we consider the system to be at a moment t of the weakening process of the alliance where the system is out of its stability space—the alliance dissolves when the competitive (negative) circles re-appear in the system. On the way, before the system reaches the dissolution, transitional stable coalitions are possible while the system is still in the stability space.

4 Two Cases of Dissolution

We focus here on the dissolution of a global alliance that has previously created stability. When the dissolution occurs, the incentive effect of the initial global concept vanishes for this particular alliance. This makes the negative circuits of the primary propensities between the respective countries to be again instrumental in their respective search for optimization.

Two different effects of the dissolution can be distinguished: (1) the instability involving all the countries; (2) the instability affecting only part of the system—the countries of the dissolved coalition leading to semi-stability. We illustrate below the two cases with historical examples.

4.1 Dissolution of the Global Alliances in Syria—An Unstable System

Syria includes many different ethnic and religious communities unified under one government by the French mandate. While Sunnis, Druzes, Alawites (a branch of Shia), Shiits, and Christians are the largest religious communities of Syria, the Alawite minority has occupied most of the key government and military positions. The politics is exclusively based on cronyism, which is characteristic of the entire East, so that the Alawite community and their allies get a good part of the political and economic benefits.

The religious composition of Syria is schematically illustrated in Figure 3a showing the original propensities as they appeared in the beginning of the twentieth century. Several conflicting (negative) circles are present in the system, so that the system does not have a rational stability, a stable optimal configuration.

Today's conflict in Syria exhibits a sharpest split between the ruling Alawite minority and the country's poor religious periphery—Sunni majority mostly aligned with the opposition where the prosperous part of the Syrian people for whom religion is not of an absolute vital importance passes from one side to another.

As stated in several historical sources (Fisher 2013; Escobar 2012), the problem is rooted in socio-economic dimensions, rather than in the religious context. Those different religious communities find themselves united under conditions of extreme poverty with neither economic nor social

safety prospect, as opposed to the prosperity of the governing class. Such a discrepancy has fueled the civil uprising.

It is worth underlining that in the second half of the twentieth century, the Syrian stability has been settled by the materialization of a global alliance calling against a common enemy, the newly created state of Israel. The global alliance, denoted by *I*, has unified the frustrated population of Syria. The alliance has neutralized all the antagonistic communities, in contrast to the Israeli success in unification of its different ethnic and religious branches, were not able to come up with their own autonomy. The alliance *I* is shown in Figure 3b.

In the beginning of the twenty-first century, Egypt, Tunisia, and Libya came up with a public protest against their present regimes. The uprising against the government in Egypt and Tunisia was quick and decisive. In Libya the protest led to a short civil war that induced the overthrow of the government. Those examples inspired the resistance and rebellion of the unfavored Syrian population, which has been suffering from social and economic inequalities.

The social awakening led to the dissolution of the anti-Israel global alliance, freeing the powerful instabilities of the internal conflicts. A new global alliance, denoted by *B*, has installed immediately in opposition to the government of Bashar al-Assad with the simultaneous forming of the opposite alliance, which supported the regime (see Figure 3c). The opposition has attracted together most of the Sunnis and a large part of the Druze community. The global alliance *B* splits the population into two parts so that the system is stabilized, as shown in the figure (all the circles are positive).

However, division of Syria into two opposite alliances could not produce a stable configuration. As soon as the current

Figure 3: Dissolution of the global alliances in Syria

(a) The figure shows schematically the original system of Syria's largest religious communities in the beginning of the twentieth century. Here, the primary negative propensities are highlighted with blue while the positive propensities are marked with black. As we can see, there are several conflicting (negative) circles in the system. The system does not have a rational stability, a stable optimal configuration.

(b) A system of Syrian religious communities in the 1970s under the anti-Israel state global *I*. The antagonistic communities, which have not come up with their own autonomy, were unified into a stable coalition based on the ethical considerations. The new cooperative propensities are highlighted with bold green.

(c) A system of Syrian communities since 2010. The new conflicting propensities are highlighted with bold blue. The opposition's global alliance *B* has attracted, together with most of the Sunnis, a part of the Druze community. All the circles in the system are positive, so the global alliance splits the population into two religious stable parts.

To view the electronic version of this journal and this image, scan the code below or visit:
http://www.ipsonet.org/publications/open-access/policy-and-complex-systems/
volume-1-number-1-spring-2014

conflict will be resolved, the alliance B will naturally dissolve and the original ethnics and religious frustrations will be again active, thus fueling new instabilities.

It should be noted that in reality the Syrian system is larger and more complex accommodating many minor religious communities and some large communities made up of several different ethnic groups that often disfavor each other. An example can be Kurds and native Syrian Arabs who belong to the Sunnis community. Nevertheless, the system of religious communities presented in the above example provides a simplified picture, which already exhibits the main instabilities and the complexity of the Syrian conflict.

It should be noted that in reality the Syrian system is larger and more complex accommodating many minor religious communities and some large communities made up of several different ethnic groups that often disfavor each other. An example can be Kurds and native Syrian Arabs who belong to the Sunnis community. Nevertheless, the system of religious communities presented in the above example provides a simplified picture, which already exhibits the main instabilities and the complexity of the Syrian conflict.

4.2 Dissolution of The Soviet Global Alliance—A Semi-Stable System

The case of a semi-stable system, a system where one of the coalitions remains stable while the other fluctuates due to the dissolution of the corresponding global alliance, can be illustrated with the collapse of the Soviet alliance.

In the middle of the last century, the Eastern alliance represented by the Warsaw Pact and the Western alliance represented by NATO were the leading opposing global alliances in Europe. In the seventh decade of its existence, the Soviet Union, which held the Warsaw Pact nations together, mainly by the military–political factor, collapsed after the Warsaw Pact was dissolved. This event led to the dissolution of the entire Eastern alliance and, as a result, to the fragmentation of the Soviet coalition, dropping back the formerly unified countries into their respective primary ethnic hostility. In contrast to the Eastern sector, the coalition of NATO remained stable.

Figure 4 illustrates schematically the main features of the systems made up of Soviet and NATO countries with the collapse of the Soviet global alliance. In both sides negative triangles can be identified as for instance Georgia–Armenia–Russia on the Soviet side and Germany–Italy– France on the NATO side.

To highlight the associated phenomena we present the case of three countries on each side denoted respectively by $\{1_S, 2_S, 3_S\}$ for both the Soviet part and the Far East countries and by $\{4_N, 5_N, 6_N\}$ for the Western Europe part. Intermediary countries of Eastern Europe such as Yugoslavia and Bosnia are denoted by $\{7_I\}$.

Primarily, before the Soviet concept has been implemented in the region, the system of countries $\{1_S, 2_S, 3_S, 4_N, 5_N, 6_N, 7_I\}$ formed two independent groups each having negative circuits of propensities, as shown in Figure 4a. Then, the Soviet global alliance S and the opposing NATO global alliance N were established.

In our illustration, the countries' natural belongings were distributed as follows. Countries $\{1_S, 2_S, 3_S\}$ as well as 7_I belonged to S, while $\{4_N, 5_N, 6_N\}$ belonged to N. The resulting externally induced interactions are shown in Figure 4b in bold font. The associated additional propensities stabilize the originally unstable systems into two opposing coalitions $\{1_S, 2_S, 3_S, 7_I\}$ and $\{4_N, 5_N, 6_N\}$.

Note that country 7_I having no significant impact on the i_S -countries initially happens to belong naturally to the Soviet global alliance S. Due to the new interactions, 7_I is detached from the N countries with which it was associated initially through a positive mutual bond and as such is attached to the S-coalition.

Here, the S-coalition holds the intermediary country 7_I only due to the attraction of the global alliance S. As soon as the Soviet alliance collapses, the country joined the N -coalition adjusting to its best configuration as shown in Figure 4c. The countries of the former Soviet coalition turn back to their respective initial negative propensities. However, the fluctuations of those countries do not affect the stable N-coalition for which the cooperative character of the interactions has persisted prevailing its stability. The overall system is thus semi-stable.

The intermediary countries are those disconnected or weakly connected to the Soviet Union. Those countries served as "isolators" between the two opponent coalitions, which impeded the instability of the Eastern side to propagate to the Western one. Among those countries were Hungary, Czech Republic, Poland, Yugoslavia, Czechoslovakia, Bosnia, and other countries of Northern and Eastern Europe. In 1999, the first three of them were invited to join NATO. Membership has been expanded later to several Northern and Eastern European countries which then gained a new stability. In contrast, the Caucasian region on the Eastern side till today shows high instability.

4.3 Remarks on the Modeling of Dissolution

It is worth remarking that within the context of rational instability where the countries as fully rational actors can assume possible losses at maximization; the semi-stability is only possible when the system consists of two disconnected (or weakly connected, i.e., connected by negligible bond values) parts.

Modeling of the Soviet global alliance dissolution has already been discussed in Galam (2002) by connecting the decent of the global alliance exchanges to a change in the value of the countries' natural belonging parameter. Subsequent affiliation to NATO by some Eastern Europe countries was explained by reversing their natural disposition.

Although such a scenario provides an explanation for both the instability driven by the dissolution and the renewed stability in some specific part of the Eastern Europe, it contradicts the fact that the countries' natural dispositions are the result of a long historical process and cannot be modified at the will of a government. Instead, considering new well-designed global alliances seems to be more appropriate. In addition it could allow bringing in novel stable coalitions among the problematic regions such as Caucasus.

The above illustrations are typical examples of dissolution where a unique factor of interest allows each country to interact on the associated single dimension of the respective global alliance. It is a uni-factor stability process.

In contrast, the multi-factor stability process implies an equiprobable influence of both opposing global alliances on the countries. As we can see in Formula (6) for the total propensity in multi-factor form, both global alliances concurrently contribute to the new interactions between the countries and, thereby, to the stability of the coalitions.

Since the weakening of global alliance M, with any country i naturally be-

Figure 4: Dissolution of the Soviet global alliance

(a) Initial system prior to the formation of global alliances with 1_S, 2_S, 3_S and for the Soviet part and the Far East countries, 4_N, 5_N, 6_N for Western Europe countries and 7_I for the intermediary countries of Eastern Europe. All bonds are the historical ones. The negative propensities are highlighted with bright blue.

(b) The Soviet S and the opposing NATO N global alliances have induced interactions that stabilized the system into two opposing coalitions $\{1_S, 2_S, 3_S, 7_I\}$ and $\{4_N, 5_N, 6_N\}$. The globally induced interactions are highlighted in green bold font.

(c) As a result of the Soviet alliance's dissolution, the countries of the former Soviet coalition turn back to the initial negative propensities. Intermediary countries served as "isolators" between the two former opponent coalitions. Later, the country gradually joined the N-coalition adjusting to their best configuration. The fluctuations of the former Soviet countries do not affect the stable N-coalition where the cooperative character of the interactions has persisted. The outcome is a semi-stable system.

To view the electronic version of this journal and this image, scan the code below or visit:
http://www.ipsonet.org/publications/open-access/policy-and-complex-systems/
volume-1-number-1-spring-2014

longing to it, is determined through the following change in the i's propensities:

$$p_{ij}^{\ total}(t) = J_{ij} + \alpha^i(t)\, p_{ij}^{\ G} + p_{ij}^{\ K} \quad (9)$$

the dissolution of a global alliance in the multi-factor stability will have a weaker effect on the stable coalitions than the dissolution in the uni-factor case.

This effect comes from the fact that when contributions from one global alliance dismiss, coalitions may remain stable due to contributions from the opposing stable alliance. The co-existence of attraction to the opposing alliances concurrently on multiple factors may thus dramatically improve the robustness of the stability.

It can be noted that the multi-factor setting in coalition forming corresponds to countries with democratic form of government. The stability in those settings is a priori more robust and resistant to the dissolution. In contrast, the uni-factor stability appears to be linked to authoritarian form of government where one of the opposing groups solely dictates over the country's interest. For this reason, the authoritarian structures tend to collapse suddenly, bringing thereby extensive instability followed by a burst of ongoing conflicts.

In this frame, the dissolution of the Soviet side is a dramatic example. Soviet alliance represented an authoritarian regime where the communist countries, on any factors of their interest, were focused on the Soviet ideology. The political dictatorship was reinforced by a centralized economic support. When the alliance dismissed, the coalition collapsed at once with the simultaneous loss of the influence that the ideology has held over all the Eastern Europe including the Caucasian region.

Comparing the stability conditions (5) and (6) for the uni-factor and the multi-factor stabilization correspondingly, it appears that in the first case the condition must be satisfied for the amplitudes from a unique factor and in the second one, it must be satisfied for several independent factors simultaneously. Therefore the stability is easier to attain within the authoritarian than within the democratic settings. At the same time, as we have seen, once the stability is reached, it is more solid within the democratic settings. This conclusion is coherent with several historical events from the past and also from the recent times (Linz and Alfred 2011; Rutherford 2013).

5 Conclusion

Due to the evolutionary changes in the system's environment, a global alliance which has sustained a stable coexistence with an opposing alliance may dissolve. Such changes produce an attenuation of the interactions between the countries previously motivated by this alliance and reveal the primary propensities between the countries. When the circuits of bonds are negative the dissolution produces an instability.

For actors with limited rationality— the ones that are unable to foresee improvements beyond a limited number of intermediate steps, such negative circuit may produce no changes with regard to the stability of the coalitions. However, for countries which are fully rational, the dissolution may result in one of two utter cases of instability.

The first one is when the instability propagates to the stable coalition and the entire system goes into instability. The second one is when the unstable part disconnects as a result of the dissolution from the stable one, and the system is divided into stable and unstable parts. Various historical cases illustrate the situation, some of which are the recent conflicts in Syria and the collapse of the Soviet Union.

In the frame of the global alliance model, re-stabilization of the resulting unstable system can be achieved by emergence of new global alliances able to bring in effective interactions to yield new stable coalitions. For countries of the former Soviet alliance, those may be global alliances that incite and put the focus on economical interactions. Some efforts in this direction are being made today by the former Soviet countries.

For Syria, the key of governing may be shifted from the traditional ethnic-religious key to the Statehood key, which refers to the process of constructing a national identity focusing on social safety and prosperity, as it has been achieved in some Eastern countries.

References

Axelrod, R., and D.S. Bennett. 1993. "A Landscape Theory of Aggregation." *British Journal Political Sciences* 23: 211-233.

Escobar, P. 2012. Syria's Pipelineistan War. *Aljazeera*, 08/2012.

Fisher, M. 2013. Syria: What You Need To Know, *World*, 09/2013.

Florian, R., and S. Galam. 2000. "Optimizing Conflicts in the Formation of Strategic Alliances." *European Physics Journal B* 16: 189-194.

Galam, S. 1996. "Fragmentation Versus Stability in Bimodal Coalitions." *Physica A* 230: 174-188.

Galam, S. 1998. "Comment on a Landscape Theory of Aggregation." *British Journal Political Sciences* 28: 411-412.

Galam, S. 2002. "Spontaneous Coalition Forming. Why Some Are Stable?," In ACRI 2002, LNCS 2493, eds. S. Bandini, B. Chopard, and M. Tomassini. Berlin Heidelberg: *Springer-Verlag*, 1-9.

Galam, S., Y. Gefen, and Y. Shapir. 1982. "Sociophysics: A New Approach of Sociological Collective Behavior." *British Journal Political Sciences* 9: 1-13.

Gerardo, G.N., F. Samaniego-Steta, M. del Castillo-Mussot, and G.J. Vazquez. 2007. "Three- Body Interactions in Sociophysics and their Role in Coalition Forming." *Physica A* 379: 226-234.

Kotkin, S. 2003. *Armageddon Averted: The Soviet Collapse, 1970—2000*. Oxford University Press.

Linz, J.J., and S. Alfred. 2011. *Problems of Democratic Transition and Consolidation: Southern Europe, South America, and Post-communist Europe, 1970-2000*. JHU Press.

Matthews, R. 2000. "A Spin Glass Model of Decisions in Organizations." In *Business Research Yearbook*, eds. G. Biberman, and A. Alkhafaji. Saline, Michigan: McNaughton and Gunn, 7, 6.

Rutherford, B.K. 2013. *Egypt After Mubarak: Liberalism Islam, and Democracy in the Arab World*. Princeton University Press.

Tim Hatamian, G. 2005. On Alliance Prediction by Energy Minimization, Neutrality and Separation of Players, arxiv.org/pdf/physics/0507017.

Vinogradova, G., and S. Galam. 2012. "Rational Instability in the Natural Coalition Forming." *Physica A: Statistical Mechanics and its Applications* 392 (2013): 60256040.

Vinogradova, G., and S. Galam. 2013. The Stabilizing Role of Global Alliances in the Dynamics of Coalition Forming, arxiv.org/abs/1311.3900.

The Price of Big Science: Saturation or Abundance in Scientific Publishing?

Caroline S. Wagner, Ph.D.[A], Dae Joong Kim[B]

Science policymaking is facing a rapidly changing landscape. Rapid growth and globalization of science are complicated by the proliferation of venues for publications, which continue to grow in number at an exponential rate. The growth rate is nullifying the hypothesis about its trajectory put forth by Derek de Solla Price (1961 and 1963); he suggested that science would reach a saturation point. In fact, the current system is proliferating, not just in numbers of published articles but also in the geographic location where knowledge is produced and in the types of venues for output (such as open source). The knowledge production system shares features with complex systems, so we propose a complex systems model to test the hypothesis. The model is designed along a stock and flow relationship between knowledge creation and obsolescence that tracks closely with actual numbers. The model further suggests that the publication system will continue to see exponential growth, and with this, may have experienced a phase shift from operating under conditions of scarcity to one of abundance. Abundant systems are characterized by openness, collaboration, and sharing—all features seen in contemporary science. Policymakers may need to shift policy toward scanning and integrating abundant knowledge to account for its proliferation and distribution across the growing knowledge landscape.

Keywords: science policy; knowledge production; complex systems modeling; collaboration

Introduction

The output of public investment in science and technology is contained in published articles, notes, and letters in scientific journals. These communications can be assumed to be part of a communications system with dynamics. The system has features of complex systems in that it is nonlinear, it has multiple agents competing for resources, and the resulting organization is emergent. Policymakers would like to understand, predict, measure, and control the processes in order to ensure that benefits accrue to intended beneficiaries. The complex system of scientific publication remains poorly understood, however. This article addresses this gap.

The eco-system of scientific communications has a number of levels, including

---

[A] Dr. Caroline S. Wagner holds the Ambassador Milton A. and Roslyn Z. Wolf Chair in International Affairs at the John Glenn School of Public Affairs, The Ohio State University, Columbus, OH. She earned her doctorate from the University of Amsterdam in Science and Technology Dynamics, her Master of Arts degree in Science, Technology and Public Policy from George Washington University, and a Bachelor of Arts from Trinity College, Washington, DC.

[B] Dae Joong Kim is a lecturer at Dongguk University in the Republic of Korea. Mr. Kim is a specialist in complex systems and public policy.

researchers operating largely within academic institutions. Researchers span institutional boundaries to self-organize into disciplines. Disciplinary organization is stabilized within journals reporting on activities within the field. Funding agencies also largely organize along disciplinary lines. Funding is based upon past publication performance and excellence as measured by citations to previous work in high impact journals.

Various attempts have been made to measure the scope and trajectory of scientific publishing, although not in ways that reveal systemic features. The literature on the growth of science has counted the number of articles and the proliferation of journals and other venues (such as online journals) where science is published. The rise of new venues of publication—such as arXiv, the Public Library of Science (PLoS), and Scientific Commons—complicates the counting and categorization processes. On the one hand, it shows vitality within scientific research, and on the other, it challenges those policymakers who rely on databases such as Web of Science and Scopus, which, for all their strengths, are limited in their ability to represent the scope of scientific output (Larsen and Von Ins 2010; Stevan Harnad 1997; Christine Borgman, Wallis, and Enyedy 2007). The databases are highly skewed toward reporting elite science rather than all of the scientific outputs.

Price's hypothesis of growth of scientific knowledge

The rapid growth of science is not new: even in the seventeenth century, scholars bemoaned the problem of keeping up with the rush of publications. In 1613, Barnaby Rich wrote: "One of the diseases of this age is the multiplicity of books! They doth so overcharge the world that it is not able to digest the abundance of idle matter that is every day hatched and brought forth into the world." In an attempt to characterize contemporary science, most scholars turn to the seminal work of Derek de Solla Price, who began his studies of science in the early 1960s. In this case, we will test Price's hypothesis—tied to the "Big Science" model—of the saturation point of scientific publishing. In 1961, Price pointed out that scientific output had been growing at an exponential rate for three centuries. He further noted that the laws of physics would suggest that nothing can continue to grow indefinitely along an exponential growth curve. With this in mind, Price proposed a saturation point, shown in Figure 1, where he hypothesized that the growth trend of scientific publication would follow an s-curve in that knowledge would reach a saturation point. He anticipated that this point would occur within a generation from his writing (which would be contemporaneous with this article) and then would level off. The growth of scientific knowledge would reach a point where its growth would shift from exponential to a steady state of production.

To support his argument, Price analyzed the total number of papers published in scientific fields since 1740. Based on the historical trend of the published papers, the finite nature of growth, and the known numbers at the time of calculation, Price expected that science would reach a point where exponential growth was no longer possible. Price's thesis and associated literature has been well reviewed by many scholars, including Jinha (2010), Lariviere, Archambault, and Gingras (2008) and Fernandez-Cano, Torralbo, and Vallejo (2004). Lariviere, Archambault, and Gingras (2008) reviewed the literature on the lifecycle of scientific literature. They calculated Price's Index (1986) of knowledge obsolescence for

To view the electronic version of this journal and this image, scan the code below or visit:
http://www.ipsonet.org/publications/open-access/policy-and-complex-systems/
volume-1-number-1-spring-2014

Figure 1. Price's knowledge saturation model
Source: Price (1960)

100 years of publications in Web of Science based on citations. They show that even with the rapid increase in output, knowledge is not becoming obsolete more rapidly. Moreover, the average age of cited literature has held fairly stable at eight years for nearly 50 years (p. 295). They calculate Price's Index (1963) of obsolescence and found that the Internet may be enabling greater access to older literature, which in turn is being cited. They infer that this access may be slowing the rate of obsolescence.

Similarly, Jinha (2010) found that scientific output has kept growing exponentially from the time that Price conducted his calculations. Jinha (2010) investigated annual global research output patterns based on the amount of accumulated scientific articles between 1726 and 2009 and found that the growth of publications at the article level is growing along the pure exponential growth curve in Price's model in Figure 1, not along Price's saturation curve[1] (see appendix). Table 1 shows supporting data.

As Price himself noted in later works (1986), electronic formats and storage capabilities have presented to science the enormous potential to manage and develop databases in formats that did not exist when he first proposed the saturation hypothesis. The advent of the Internet provides the ability to create new electronic journals and new forms of data storage. Whether directly related to the Internet or to other dynamics or some combination in between, scientific knowledge in terms of articles as well as venues (journals and online sites) is growing

at a significant rate without having reached Price's anticipated saturation point. Indeed, Larsen and Von Ins (2010)[2] find that traditional scientific publishing (publication in peer-reviewed journals) has not given way to online publishing, and is still increasing, although with some notable differences between fields in growth rates.

Why is scientific publishing not "saturated"?

We explored the question of why scientific knowledge has not reached the saturation point Price anticipated. Perhaps the most obvious reason is the emergence of electronic storage and diffusion technologies. In 1960, paper libraries imposed physical constraints that limited the ability of scientists to access and build upon earlier work. These limitations have been overcome or at least mitigated[3] with the advent of digital abstracting and publishing, including the creation of online resources and the rise of open access journals; the access to archives of formerly unpublished, primary source materials now available online; and massive electronic storage capacity (with anticipated access to full text still somewhat limited). Moreover, it would not have been obvious to Price that, by the twenty-first century, developing countries would rapidly join the ranks of scientific research, and further, that their researchers would seek publication outlets at the same rate as those in advanced countries (Wagner and Wong, 2011).

---

[1] Among those scholars who have tried to count the numbers of articles and journals being published in one year or accumulative over time, the estimates range fairly widely depending upon the assumptions about the boundaries of scientific scholarship, as well as the database from which the analysts draw.

[2] Larsen and Von Ins analyzed available data between 1907 and 2007 from a number of literature databases, including Science Citation Index (SCI) and Social Sciences Citation Index (SSCI).

[3] Some say that the continuing practice of having scientific articles behind the 'walls' of subscription-based journals limits access for many potential readers, see Harnad (2007).

To view the electronic version of this journal and this image, scan the code below or visit: http://www.ipsonet.org/publications/open-access/policy-and-complex-systems/volume-1-number-1-spring-2014

Table 1. Data underlying assumptions for revisiting Price's model

To view the electronic version of this journal and this image, scan the code below or visit: http://www.ipsonet.org/publications/open-access/policy-and-complex-systems/volume-1-number-1-spring-2014

Figure 2. Research outputs in numbers of articles, 1726–2009

The quality of the expanding output is a significant question that has not gone without comment, even by Derek Price himself, as well as philosophers of science, Robert Merton, Thomas Kuhn, and Karl Popper. Indeed, Popper (1976) viewed the growth of scientific output as a deficiency of science, since, in his view, the "growth of knowledge… is not a repetitive or cumulative process, but one of error elimination…" (p.144) and therefore should not increase in volume, but decrease as errors are eliminated from the understanding of the natural world. Price also wrestled with the quality question, noting that perhaps it would be better to take a different approach to science: "One may study the growth of only important discoveries, inventions, and scientific laws, rather than all such things…" (1961, p. 32), thus reducing the overall output of science.

Indeed, several philosophers of science have suggested that science should be conducted by an elite group of highly talented researchers, rather than a broad group. Bradford's Law (Garfield 1971) informed the earliest efforts by Francis Narin, Eugene Garfield, and Henry Small to identify high quality science and are based upon the premise that a small percentage of output would represent the highest quality work; thus a limited dataset would constitute the bulk of material worth tracking (Garfield 1976). (This is justification for the limited number of journals indexed in the Web of Science.)[4]

The question of how quality is measured and what is included in different databases is beyond the scope of this paper. We have the more modest goal of understanding scientific knowledge growth as part of a project to study why scientific collaboration (as measured by co-authorships) continues to grow. To address the question of expectations about the growth of science and why it has exceeded hypothetical expectations, we developed a systems model as to whether scientific publishing operates a complex system (Katz 2006). Showing that scientific publishing operates as a complex system (rather than simply as an aggregation of lists that continues to grow exponentially) would provide us with a set of conditions upon which we could test, understand, and further study the system for additional research. The following discussion presents the model and initial findings.

Scientific publishing has many features in common with complex systems[5] which lead us to make this measure. The features in common include the dynamic growth of output, the emergent nature of that output, the openness of the system in accepting inputs, and the self-organization of researchers into disciplines and collaborative teams. Complex systems are dynamic and have a propensity to exhibit scaling properties along a power law form. These scaling properties appear to be a feature of scientific publication, at least in co-authorship (Wagner and Leydesdorff 2005) and in citation behavior (Katz 2000). Table 2 compares features of complex systems with features of scientific knowledge production whose statistical features have been shown by Lotka (1929), Price (1963), and others (Katz 2000) to display similarities with other complex systems.

To further test this systems hypothesis and to explain why Price's theory of growth cannot be upheld, we constructed

---

[4] Estimates have been made of the extent of scientific publication within and outside of SCIE. Bjork, Roos and Lauri estimate 2008 and Wagner and Wong's (2011) calculation suggest that the extent of scientific publication outside SCIE may be considerably larger when the publications of developing countries are fully counted.

[5] (Baranger, n.d.).

an explanatory and predictive model about why and how scientific knowledge (with publication as a proxy for knowledge) is created, diffused, and accumulated, making no other assumptions about quality.

Modeling

System dynamics enables an approach to modeling structures and simulating behaviors in cases where a structure or complex phenomena emerges. We constructed a theoretical, testable model of creation, diffusion, and accumulation and obsolescence of scientific knowledge. The system[6] can be modeled as the relationship between stock and flow. Stock is conceptualized as accumulation of knowledge, which increases (or decreases) over time. The magnitude of stock is influenced by flow (inflow or outflow) over time. Relationships of such stock and flow are visualized within system dynamics as shown in Figure 4.

The stock and flow model includes the following:

- Stock, inflow, and outflow are the main variables in the structure of system.
- The stock of scientific knowledge is determined by the inflow and outflow process.
- The system is influenced by various auxiliary variables such as initial quantity, creation rate, and obsolescence rate of the stock of scientific knowledge.
- New scientific knowledge is produced by drawing upon existing scientific knowledge (which can be different or

similar knowledge).
- Additional scientific knowledge is stored and adds to and replaces some scientific knowledge.
- The inflow is the combination of the recombination of existing scientific knowledge and the creation rate.
- The outflow is decided by the obsolescence rate (or death rate).
- The death rate is decided by the stock of scientific knowledge and its average life.

This scientific knowledge growth model is very similar to population growth models based on births, living persons, and deaths, which is a traditional system dynamics model. The population is the agglomeration of the number of births as inflow, the current stock of people, and the number of deaths as outflow, just as scientific knowledge consists of all the new information, accepted scientific theory along with active research, minus the scientific knowledge that no longer remains actively used or exchanged. (One key difference in the knowledge model is that some 'obsolete' knowledge could be revived to contribute to the system, which have been discussed in the literature as 'sleeping beauties' (Van Raan 2004) but might also be called 'zombies.') Scientific knowledge is normalized over time: some of the normalized scientific knowledge becomes generalized; and some of it disappears. In these respects, we can assume that scientific knowledge repeats this process over time with an accumulation. Based on basic assumptions, a stock-flow system model of scientific knowledge growth is constructed as seen in Figure 4.

---

[6] A system is a set of entities (called the elements of the system) mutually related in such a way that the state of each element determines and/or is determined by the state of some other element or elements, and every element is connected by the state of some other element or elements, and every element is connected to every other by a chain of such elements. A system as a whole has a function only if it is an element in a more inclusive system, that is, only if it affects something other than itself. (Self-perpetuation does not count as a function in this sense.)

To view the electronic version of this journal and this image, scan the code below or visit:
http://www.ipsonet.org/publications/open-access/policy-and-complex-systems/
volume-1-number-1-spring-2014

Table 2. Scientific publishing as a complex system

To view the electronic version of this journal and this image, scan the code below or visit:
http://www.ipsonet.org/publications/open-access/policy-and-complex-systems/
volume-1-number-1-spring-2014

Figure 3. Flow and stock diagram

To view the electronic version of this journal and this image, scan the code below or visit:
http://www.ipsonet.org/publications/open-access/policy-and-complex-systems/
volume-1-number-1-spring-2014

Figure 4. Causal model of stock and flow of knowledge

In the progress of science, there is some knowledge that is not superseded or nullified, no matter how many publications are published. The core knowledge is no longer cited. Thus, the box "knowledge" in Figure 4 assumes that some core human knowledge remains stable. The model shows causal relationships among variables whose interaction creates system dynamics. The system determines a behavior regarding scientific knowledge growth. The relationships between knowledge growth and its behavior can be explained in two structural features—stock and flow, and feedback loop. First, the knowledge growth can be explained as a function between net creation rate and initial knowledge as seen in Equations 1 and 2. The input of new scientific knowledge creates growth of scientific knowledge in the system which is stored, and it replaces other scientific knowledge in the Popperian sense of eliminating error or confirming earlier findings. Thus, some knowledge experiences 'obsolescence' in the sense that it is no longer cited even though a small percentage becomes part of normalized knowledge. The growth of knowledge can be assumed to influence the obsolescence rate (this can also be a proxy for lower quality work) with crowding increasing the rate. In this regard, the growth of knowledge can be determined by net creation rate and initial stock of knowledge. The net creation rate is determined by the gap between creation and obsolescence rates.

Knowledge

$= INTEGRAL$ *(net creation rate, initial knowledge)*

The net creation rate is determined by the gap between creation and death rates.

net creation rate

$= creation\ rate\ (cK) - obsolescence\ rate\ (oK)$
$= (c - o)^a * K$

where c is a creation rate, o is an obsolescence rate, and a is a power value of the relationship between c and d, and K is amount of knowledge. Specifically, the pattern of scientific knowledge growth, pure exponential growth, or exponential growth with saturation can be determined by the pattern of net creation rate as seen in Figure 5. If creation dominates obsolescence (c>o) linearly (a=1) or nonlinearly (a>1), scientific knowledge will show pure exponential growth. However, if creation dominates death, and then death dominates creation like the bell-shape as seen in Figure 6, the pattern of scientific knowledge growth will show an s-shape growth (here, an exponential growth with saturation).

Scientific knowledge growth can be identified along with various feedback structures or loops around stocks and flows. Feedback structure or loops means a closed causal circle among variables. In general, there are two types of feedback structures: positive (self-reinforcement) and negative (balance). Positive feedback structures are self-reinforcing processes wherein action creates a virtuous circle. Negative feedback structure, on the other hand, is a process to stabilize or balance a system. Thus, behaviors in a system become determined by a type of feedback loop in the system. When a positive feedback dominates the whole system, the system tends to show an exponential growth. When negative feedback dominates, the system tends to show an upward or downward convex growth. An s-shape growth in a system tends to be formed when positive feedback dominates, followed by when negative feedback dominates.

In our system dynamics model, there is one positive feedback structure and two negative feedback structures as seen in Figure 5. The first positive feedback structure (R1) is the feedback loop from knowledge through creation back to knowledge.

To view the electronic version of this journal and this image, scan the code below or visit:
http://www.ipsonet.org/publications/open-access/policy-and-complex-systems/
volume-1-number-1-spring-2014

Figure 5. Exponential growth versus saturation levels on Price's saturation curve

The quantity of creation is determined by knowledge and creation rate positively reinforcing one another, and the size of knowledge is determined by the size of creation. In other words, the larger the knowledge the larger the creation, the larger the creation rate the larger the creation capacity, and the larger the creation capacity the larger the knowledge quantity. This feedback structure makes a self-reinforcing loop that grows scientific knowledge continuously.

There is a negative feedback loop (B1) to control the pace of knowledge growth. The negative feedback structure is the feedback loop from knowledge through normal obsolescence and obsolescence back to knowledge. Knowledge can and does become obsolescent at some point. When scientific knowledge is obsolete, articles are no longer cited. The obsolete scientific knowledge negatively influences knowledge growth. The pace of obsolescence is influenced by the normal obsolescent rate positively. In other words, the larger the normal obsolescence rate, the larger the amount of obsolescent material. However, the normal obsolescence rate is influenced by the average lifetime of scientific knowledge negatively; that is, the longer average lifetime of knowledge the fewer the normal obsolescence rate. In this respect, this negative feedback structure tends to set the pace of knowledge growth.

The size of obsolescence is also influenced by the effect of knowledge crowding on obsolescence as seen in the negative feedback loop (B2). This loop is formed by causal relationships among knowledge, normalized knowledge, effect of knowledge crowding on obsolescence, and obsolescence. Through the loop, we can see how scientific knowledge becomes obsolescent. Normalized scientific knowledge is determined by the function *(f)=knowledge/carrying capacity*. In other words, scientific

knowledge and carrying capacity influence the formation of normalized knowledge positively and negatively, respectively. Kuhn (1962) suggested that within the structure of scientific revelations, the stock of scientific knowledge is normalized. We accept this view; the stock is the carrying capacity of knowledge among scientists in the system plus codified knowledge. Thus, in our model, we assume that scientific knowledge repeats this process over time with an accumulation. In addition, the normalized knowledge is assumed to have a nonlinear relationship with its effect on obsolescence over time. Obsolescence is expected to increase more quickly than knowledge as knowledge grows to a level of quantity (that we do not determine in this experiment). In measurable systems, it is difficult to express the relationship between them as a constant value and it may be that the value is not constant, although we did not test for this fact.

The type of feedback loop (positive or negative feedback loop) will determine the direction of the growth of the scientific knowledge system. The dynamics will determine whether the system displays exponential growth or s-shape growth. In other words, when the positive feedback structure (R1) dominates the other two negative feedback structures (B1 and B2) in our knowledge system, it creates an exponential growth mode. The s-shape growth that Price (1963) anticipated in his scientific knowledge growth model would require negative feedback dominating at least one of the two positive feedback structures. To test the model, we constructed a simulation setting based on a stock-flow model. The simulation uses empirical data of the actual number of published articles per year between 1990 and 2010[7] as drawn from the Web of Science. Information of each parameter is described in the appendix.

Analysis

We ran the system dynamics model to match a systems model of exponential growth to actual scientific knowledge growth. The processes used are base-run simulation, extended simulation, and sensitivity analysis. In the base-run simulation model, we calibrated the simulation model with real data to see how well the assumptions about systemic features simulated within the model fit real data. Based on the results, we conducted several extended simulation analyses to estimate scientific knowledge growth direction in future. This section describes the simulations.

Base-run simulation

We first tested how accurately our system dynamics model calibrates current growth of published articles as shown in Figure 2. The simulation test output is based on real parameter information revealing a pattern very similar to that found by Jinha (2010). Simulation outputs of system dynamics as seen in Figure 6 and Table 2 show how simulated outputs are similar to actual data.

Figure 6 shows the similarity between the actual output and the simulation output per year. The dotted line represents our simulated output, and the solid line represents the actual data. When the two lines are compared, the simulation output is almost perfectly aligned with the actual data. Table 3 shows a comparison of actual growth of published articles with growth of the published articles through the

simulation numerically one by one as seen in the table. Columns 2, 5, 8, and 11 represent the number of actual published articles per year; columns 3, 6, 9, and 12 show the outputs drawn from the simulation. The simulated number of published articles in 1991 and in 2009 reached 867,769 and 1,477,664, respectively. The actual published articles in 1991 and in 2009 are 867,807 and 1,477,383, respectively. Thus, the simulation model can be shown to have enough explanatory power in tracing the current knowledge growth to validate the model.

Extended simulation

Following validation of the base-run simulation, we simulated future growth of published articles as well as growth based on Price's (1963) scientific knowledge output model. Price anticipated that scientific articles would reach a turning point to move toward the s-shape of growth after 30 years. To test Price's hypothesis, our simulation model was only extended to 2040. As a result of our model, the number of expected published articles grew to around 3.770M as seen in Figure 7. The pattern of growth can remain at the exponential rate under the current parameters.

Sensitivity analysis

We conducted a sensitivity analysis to ensure reliability and predictive power of the model under various environmental uncertainties. In simulation models, sensitivity analysis helps to build confidence by studying the

---

[7] For this aspect of testing, the annual global research output of articles investigated by Jinha (2010) draws from the pattern of scientific knowledge growth of accumulated articles between 1726 and 2009. Our simulation tested the time period between 1990 and 2010 because all real parameters between the 1726 and 1990 values could not be obtained. Thus, the base year is 1990 in our simulation model. Note that the information of each parameter is described in the appendix.

To view the electronic version of this journal and this image, scan the code below or visit:
http://www.ipsonet.org/publications/open-access/policy-and-complex-systems/
volume-1-number-1-spring-2014

Figure 6. Actual data versus base-run simulation output between 1990 and 2009

To view the electronic version of this journal and this image, scan the code below or visit:
http://www.ipsonet.org/publications/open-access/policy-and-complex-systems/
volume-1-number-1-spring-2014

Table 3. Comparison between actual outputs and simulation outputs

To view the electronic version of this journal and this image, scan the code below or visit:
http://www.ipsonet.org/publications/open-access/policy-and-complex-systems/
volume-1-number-1-spring-2014

Figure 7. Extended simulation output

uncertainties that are often associated with model parameters. Even though many parameters in system dynamics models represent quantities, it is very difficult or even impossible to measure the parameters to a high degree of accuracy in the real world. Also, some parameter values change in the real world over time (Forrester 1996). In this regard, our system dynamics model was tested to see how published article growth behavior in our system dynamics model would change after altering key parameters. The sensitivity analysis also validates the model. For analyzing sensitivity in our system dynamics, two key parameters were analyzed for the sensitivity of published article growth based on average lifetime and creation rate. The sensitivity of each parameter change was analyzed by endowing each parameter with a range as follows:

average lifetime = RANDOM UNIFORM (7, 8)

creation rate = RANDOM UNIFORM (0.30, 0.35)

where the average lifetime is assigned between seven and eight years (as found in the real world), and the growth rate is randomly unit-distributed between the fraction per year 0.30 and 0.35. Also, where:
(1) Change current (fractional) creation rate, 0.325 up to 0.35 or down to 0.30 in the year 2009 to see what the published article growth would be in future. Growth patterns of published articles appeared as seen in Figure 8. When the creation rate was up to 0.35, the number of published articles became 5.774M; on the other hand, when the creation rate was down to 0.30, the number of published articles became 1.671M. Thus, this output shows that published article growth could be more sensitive when it was down than when it was up. We can see that the scientific knowledge output growth would be considerably daunted when

creation rate was down, but it still shows a growth pattern.

(2) Change the current parameter value regarding average lifetime, 7.5 years up to 8.0 years, or down to 7.0 years in the year 2009 to see what the published article growth would be in the future. Growth patterns of published articles appeared as seen in Figure 9. When the average lifetime was up to eight years, the number of published articles became 6.737M; on the other hand, when the average lifetime was down to seven years, the number of published articles became 1.905M. This output shows that published article growth could be more sensitive when it is up than when it is down.

(3) Conduct sensitivity analysis by considering changes of both creation rate and average lifetime. The graph in Figure 9 shows the behavior of published article growth when the two parameters are changed at the same time.

The current extended simulation line is based on the parameter values creation rate = 0.35, and average lifetime = 7.5. At the extended simulation line, there exist four confidence bounds (50%, 75%, 95%, and 100%) for all the output values of published article growth shown in Figure 10. These bounds were generated when the two parameters were randomly varied around their distributions at the same time. From this sensitivity analysis, we can expect that the growth of published articles would show a purely exponential growth rate, especially when each parameter was changed to an upper value. However, when the parameters, creation rate and average lifetime were lowered below the current parameter values, the published article growth does not follow a purely exponential growth pattern.

To view the electronic version of this journal and this image, scan the code below or visit:
http://www.ipsonet.org/publications/open-access/policy-and-complex-systems/
volume-1-number-1-spring-2014

Figure 8. Sensitivity analysis: what if creation rate was up or down

To view the electronic version of this journal and this image, scan the code below or visit:
http://www.ipsonet.org/publications/open-access/policy-and-complex-systems/
volume-1-number-1-spring-2014

Figure 9. Sensitivity analysis: adjusting average lifetime up or down

To view the electronic version of this journal and this image, scan the code below or visit: http://www.ipsonet.org/publications/open-access/policy-and-complex-systems/ volume-1-number-1-spring-2014

Figure 10. Sensitivity analysis: adjusting creation rate and average lifetime change up or down

Conclusion

The rate of production of scientific publications appears to be continuing on an exponential growth curve[8] against the prediction of Derek de Solla Price. (This article examines only publications, but it has been noted that scientific data (Borgman, Wallis, and Enyedy 2007) and e-Science (Hey and Trefethen 2005) are also growing phenomena, as well.) The growth of scientific publications has many possible causes, but the system itself appears to be operating efficiently. The networked nature of global science (Wagner and Leydesdorff 2005), the expansion of source materials and venues, the expansion of the practice of science to new places, the application of science to new problems (such as climate change), and the rise of China as a scientific power all may be contributing to the very rapid growth in output, increasing the complexity of the system.

The model constructed for this article suggests that scientific output may continue to grow exponentially. Many of the abstracting databases such as Web of Science (SCIE) are making an effort to grow their indexing services with the growth in the number of both journal titles and articles, but even so, the database used here contains only a portion of all publications (Wagner and Wong 2011). (Many of these non-source publications are in national languages and therefore remain difficult for us to access, but the materials are part of the corpus of science and can be expected to garner increasing attention over time.) Moreover, open access journals and other types of venues on the Internet continue to proliferate, shifting the face of scientific publishing to meet the needs of practitioners and users as well as the capacity of the tools

to deliver information. The proliferation of sources contributes to the growth trend, and also makes it more difficult to count the outputs, but we can assume that these outputs are part of the complex system of communications of science.

Others have noted the challenge to public policy of the problems of counting scientific output for national comparisons:

> It is problematic that SCI has been used and is still used as the dominant source for science indicators based on publication and citation numbers. SCI has nearly been in a monopoly situation. This monopoly is now being challenged by the new publication channels and by new sources for publication and citation counting. It is also a serious problem because a substantial amount of scientometric work and of R&D statistics has been done using a database which year for year has covered a smaller part of the scientific literature. (Larsen and Von Ins 2010, 601)

Derek de Solla Price presented the saturation hypothesis in part because exponential growth does not continue unchecked for long periods of time without one of several things happening: the physical limitations of its surroundings must change so as not to restrict growth, or the carrying capacity of the system must shift to absorb larger numbers. Both of these phenomena may be occurring. With regard to the Internet, the carrying capacity of the system has shifted to enable the absorption of new material. The rate of growth within disciplines may follow the Price's saturation curve while the rate of growth as a whole remains exponential for the near future, and this possibility needs to be tested in future research.

Price's intuition about the limits of the system in a state of exponential

---

[8] The rate of growth may not be constant; it is not possible to measure the entire system.

growth may still obtain to science but with a different interpretation. Exponential growth may have contributed to a phase shift to a new state, one characterized by abundance. Systems growing exponentially are known to reach a point of phase shift. The abundant state varies from the previous state that Price studied, where knowledge production operated within systemic features of scarcity. Paper-based output with limited availability, housed largely in the libraries of elite institutions, created conditions of a scarce system similar to biological systems scarcity.[9] The rise of electronic sharing capabilities and broader accessibility has created conditions of abundance. In systems terms, this would contribute to systemic features of openness, sharing, reciprocity, and collaboration, but also waste and redundancy, features increasingly seen in science.

Abundant knowledge challenges governance on a number of levels. Science policy has evolved under conditions of knowledge scarcity, where nations have paid for and claimed credit for the results of research physically tied to institutions. Abundance has shifted this physicality as well as accessibility, enabling practitioners with Internet access to begin to tap the vast and historic stores of scientific publications and data as they come online. The result has been both greater collaboration and the seeding of capacity in new geographic spaces. It also increases competition for use of scientific knowledge that contributes to economic growth and competitiveness.

With the insights provided by the models presented here, policymakers can predict and control variables in ways that may optimize policy effects (i.e.,

knowledge creation or diffusion). These models can be applied to improve the knowledge collaboration, increase the value of resources, and result in improved use of federal research budgets, even in a time of budgetary austerity. Efficiency can be enhanced by understanding how to integrate knowledge under conditions of abundance. This means a policy shift to track research globally (to avoid redundancy) and to increase integration opportunities. It also means supporting collaborative research opportunities in which U.S. scientists and their global counterparts work to tap knowledge in many venues.

References

Baranger, M. n.d. "Chaos, Complexity, and Entropy A Physics Talk for Non-physicists." *Entropy*, 1-17.

Björk, B., A. Roos, and M. Lauri. 2008. Global Annual Volume of Peer Reviewed Scholarly Articles and the Share Available via Different Open Access Options. *Proceedings of the ELPUB2008 Conference on Electronic Publishing*, Toronto, Canada. http://oacs.shh.fi/publications/elpub-2008.pdf

Björk, B., A. Roos, and M. Lauri. 2009. "Scientific Journal Publishing: Yearly Volume and Open Access Availability." *Information Research* 14 (1): paper 391. http://InformationR.net/ir/14-1/paper391.html

Borgman, C., J. Wallis, and N. Enyedy. 2007. "Little Science Confronts the Data Deluge: Habitat Ecology, Embedded

---

[9] Indeed, a scarce ecosystem tends to support just a few large species, some small species, and limited vegetation—consider the northern tundra as an example. The scarce knowledge system supported only a few nations conducting science, and within them, a few elite institutions that produced the majority of products.

Sensor Networks, and Digital Libraries." *International Journal on Digital Libraries* 7 (1–2): 17-30. http://www.springerlink.com/content/f7580437800m367m/?MUD=MP

Fernandez-Cano, A., M. Torralbo, and M. Vallejo. 2004. "Reconsidering Price's Model of Scientific Growth : An Overview." *Scientometrics* 61 (3): 301–321.

Forrester, J.W. 1996. "An Introduction to Sensitivity Analysis." *Course Reading Materials*, System Dynamics Self Study. MIT. http://clexchange.org/ftp/documents/Roadmaps/RM8/D-4526-2.pdf

Garfield, E. 1971. "The Mystery of the Transposed Journal Lists—Wherein Bradford's Law of Scattering is Generalized according to Garfield's Law of Concentration." *Current Contents.*

Garfield, E. 1976. "Significant Journals of Science." *Nature* 264: 609-615.

Harnad, S. 2007. Open Access Scientometrics and the UK Research Assessment Exercise. Preprint of Invited Keynote Address to *11th Annual Meeting of the International Society for Scientometrics and Informetrics.* Madrid, Spain, June 25–27, 2007. http://issi2007.cindoc.csic.es/

Hey, T., and A.E. Trefethen. 2005. "Cyberinfrastructure for e-Science." *Science* 308 (5723): 817-821.

Jinha, A. 2010. "Article 50 Million: An Estimate of the Number of Scholarly Articles in Existence." *Learned Publishing* 32 (3): 258-263.

Katz, J.S. 2000. "Scale-independent Indicators and Research Evaluation." *Science and Public Policy* 27 (1): 23-36.

Kuhn, T. 1962. *The Structure of Scientific Revolutions.* Chicago: University of Chicago Press.

Lariviere, V., E. Archambault, and Y. Gingras. 2008. "Long-Term Variation in the Aging of Scientific Literature: From Exponential Growth to Steady-State Science (1900–2004)." *Journal of The American Society For Information Science and Technology* 59 (2): 288-292.

Larsen, P.O., and M. Von Ins. 2010. "The Rate of Growth in Scientific Publication and the Decline in Coverage Provided by Science Citation Index." *Scientometrics* 84 (3): 575-603. doi:10.1007/s11192-010-0202-z

Lotka, A.J. 1929. "Biometric Functions in a Population Growing in Accordance with a Prescribed Law." *Statistics* 15: 794-798.

National Science Board. 2012. *Science and Engineering Indicators* 2012. Arlington, VA: National Science Foundation (NSB 12-01).

Popper, K. 1976. *Unended Quest; An Intellectual Autobiography.* London: Routledge.

Price, D.J.de S. 1961. *Science Since Babylon.* New Haven, CT: Yale University Press.

Price, D.J.de S. 1963. *Little Science. Big Science.* New York: Columbia University Press.

Price, D.J.de S. 1986. *Little Science, Big Science... and Beyond.* New York: Columbia University Press.

Tenopir, C.W., and D.W. King. 2009. "The Growth of Journals Publishing." In *The Future of the Academic Journal*, eds. B.

Cope, and A. Phillips. Chandos Publishing/ Woodhead Publishing Ltd. ISBN 1 84334 416 5.

Van Raan, A.F.J. 2004. "Sleeping Beauties in Science." *Scientometrics* 59 (3): 467-472.

Wagner, C.S., and L. Leydesdorff. 2005. "Network Structure, Self-organization, and the Growth of International Collaboration in Science." *Research Policy* 34 (10): 1608-1618.

Wagner, C.S., and S.K. Wong. 2011. "Unseen Science? Representation of BRICs in Global Science." *Scientometrics* 90 (3): 1001-1013.

www.ingramcontent.com/pod-product-compliance
Lightning Source LLC
Chambersburg PA
CBHW081647270326
41933CB00018B/3379